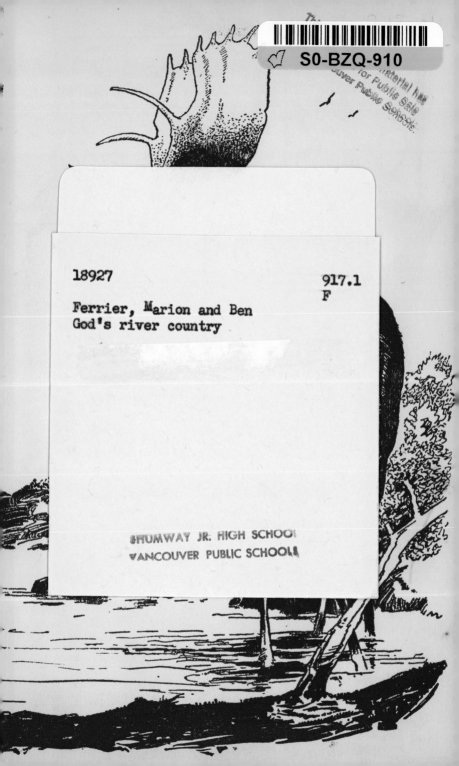

18927   917.1
                     F

Ferrier, Marion and Ben
God's river country

God's River Country

GOD'S
RIVER
COUNTRY

by Marion and Ben Ferrier

photographs by Ben Ferrier

A Lodestar Book

18927

THIS SPECIAL EDITION IS PRINTED AND DISTRIBUTED BY ARRANGEMENT WITH
THE ORIGINATORS & PUBLISHERS OF LODESTAR BOOKS, *Prentice-Hall, Inc.,* BY

E. M. HALE AND COMPANY
EAU CLAIRE, WISCONSIN

Contents

God's River Country

1

Expedition

THE TWO TALL AND HUSKY OLDER BOYS LEANING against the rail of the *S.S. Keenora* in her dock at Winnipeg guffawed when the last of our crew scrambled hastily up the gangplank, almost stumbling over their gear in their anxiety to get aboard. "Come on, Runt! Come on, Steve! Step on it. We thought you got frightened and decided not to come!"

"You're crazy," fifteen-year-old Mike said cheerfully as he thumped suitcase, camera, rod and reel, and general miscellany to the deck. "We were right on your heels. What's frightening about this trip, anyway?"

Frank and Chuck looked at each other and grinned. They were both man-sized at seventeen. "Why, son, we've told you many times . . ."

Mike snorted. "Huh! I'll wait and see. I bet you're

1

making a lot of it up. Just because you've been to the North before, you think you're big adventurers. Wild tales, that's all, wild tales!"

Steve smiled without getting into the discussion. He was not much older than Mike, but taller and broader; he was likely to be on Mike's side when the razzing started. Now he interposed calmly: "Gee, why argue? We're all after the same kind of fun."

"That," said a deep new voice, "is the kind of attitude I favor." It was Ben Ferrier, coming up behind the last arrivals. Ben was the leader of our expedition—one of the best North country guides around, a man who has made the wilderness his career and taught a good many people to see it his way.

"Hi, Chief!"

"Where is everybody? I thought we'd have a look at the map right now, since you've been pestering me for details."

"Oh boy, the route! Call roll in a loud voice, Chief," Mike suggested. "They ought to answer to their names."

Ben pulled a well-worn map from his pocket. "Losing yourself in a city or on a boat is all right—you still can tell where you are; but remember to stick with the others when we get on the trail. One of the first rules of survival."

He looked at the boys in front of him, and tried to see over the heads of the *Keenora* tourists. "Franklin Dunbaugh, Charles Nadler; O.K. Adlai Stevenson III, Charles Albright. O.K.?"

"Here!" said Frank and Chuck, Steve and Mike together.

"Where are your other Chicago sidekicks? Fred and Snarkey?"

The two other teen-agers in the crew—Frederic Hord and William K. Kellogg III—undraped themselves from a pair of deck chairs nearby and came loping.

"Did I hear my name?" "Snarkey" Kellogg was red-headed, freckled and humorous looking, entirely unsuited to his elegant name.

The Chief nodded. "I'm trying to get you all together so I only need to go over things once. The crowd's picking up; only four more to go. Why do I agree to take as many as twelve people on these outings, anyway?"

Steve reminded him, *"Five* more. Don't leave out your wife."

"It's a good thing she's tied to you," said Snarkey, and the other boys hooted and held their noses at the pun.

"Marion!" Ben boomed.

That was I. John Olmsted and Orwin Rustad and I were talking botany only twenty feet away. Scientists from the University of Minnesota, John and Orie were going along with us to make a study of plant life where no study had ever been made before. John was big and powerfully muscled. Orie, on the frail side, was already beginning to doubt his wisdom in tackling the wilderness just for the sake of science.

"Mrs. Chief, you're being paged," said John.

By the time we had pushed a few tourists aside to get to Ben and the boys, Art and Walt Eschbach had been rounded up, too. Art and Walt, a father and son team from Iowa, had taken on the job of cooking for our crew in order to get experience canoeing in Canada waters.

"Now, then!" Ben said, and unfolded the map, while all of us crowded around. "First of all, we are going down north, not up. The waterways flow down to Hudson Bay and on to the North Atlantic and the Arctic Ocean." His finger traced our route. "By boat —right now—to the north end of Lake Winnipeg and on to Norway House. There we'll launch the canoes and proceed to God's Lake by paddle and portage. Then down the God's River to York Factory on Hudson Bay, and return upstream by way of the Nelson River back to Norway House."

This would be Ben's twenty-sixth year on the canoe trails and his eighth trip guiding parties of adventurous nature-lovers through the Canadian wilderness to the Bay. For Frank and Chuck and myself, it would be the second time we had traveled the route with him. Everyone else was a greenhorn to the North country, though there were varying degrees of canoeing and camping experience among them: Art and Walt had done a great deal of canoeing on rivers in the United States, and some of the boys had learned a little at summer camps.

We weren't just going on a pleasure trip, as tourists. This was to be the real thing. We were going to travel as the Indians travel, the Crees who had taught Ben about the wilderness and given him a way of life.

Ben and I had checked and rechecked lists of supplies and voluminous duffel, and our fingers were crossed hoping we hadn't forgotten anything. Most of our gear we would pick up at Norway House; but in Winnipeg the crew had been outfitted with several pairs of mooseskin moccasins and moccasin-overs, the heavy-soled rubbers that are absolutely essential on the trail. These would be our footgear for the summer. Boots did not belong in a canoe; they were too dangerous. Everyone had also his own tumpline, which is an innocent-looking piece of leather known as a "torture strap" after the first portage.

We were to be eight weeks on the canoe trails of a vast wilderness. In a thousand miles of portaging and paddling, we would be dependent upon our own resources. At the few Hudson's Bay Company posts there would be small settlements, but we could not count on their having provisions on hand to add to our stores. Other than at these settlements, our contact with human beings would come only when and if we met a trapper or an Indian on his way to or from one of the fur trading posts. Ours was not to be a stunt of trying to prove we could live off the country. We would take with us everything we needed for the eight weeks.

Suppose that you were to make a list of everything you would need for the next two months in the way of food, bedding, clothing, shelter, and miscellaneous supplies, such as a first aid kit, reading material and toilet articles. Then multiply their total weight by the number of people in your family, say, and add to that the weight of a vehicle that would transport you, your family and these supplies on a thousand-mile journey. Even a rough estimate of the weight would leave you with a staggering total of tons and tons.

Now suppose that all of these supplies for the two months had to be unloaded every evening, reloaded every morning, and this same process repeated several times some days, with everything carried on your back from a few rods to a mile or two. About that time you would start revising the list to cut down on bulk and weight and eliminate every possible item you could live without. You would still have tons.

In the Hudson Bay area during the summer, clothing would have to be suitable for a temperature range from near freezing up to $85°$. It would have to afford protection against drenching rains and hordes of mosquitoes and black flies. Food would have to be planned to provide a balanced diet in spite of the fact that there would be no fresh or canned vegetables, no fresh or canned fruits, no fresh milk and no fresh meat except the fish we would catch. To satisfy the voracious appetites and provide energy for the tremendous physical exertion, it would be necessary to plan on consumption of at least four thousand calories per individual per day.

In this thousand miles to the Bay and return we would be traveling in a country of high winds, large lakes and tremendously fast and broad rivers. The canoes that we are accustomed to using in the United States would not be suitable or safe here. For our crew of twelve, we would use three Hudson Bay freighters, canvas covered, 19 feet long, 54 inches wide and 20 inches deep. The capacity of each is a ton of supplies plus four men.

For the whole summer we would be traveling in a country where there is more water than land, where the only highways are waterways. Our primitive means of transport would be in harmony with our surroundings. People often ask why we paddle—why we do not use an outboard motor. The answer is that a motor makes a craft a motorboat, not a canoe, despite its shape.

Now as we steamed up the lake on the way to our starting point, one of our twelve adventurers asked, "What do *you* do on the trail, Chief? Didn't you say *everybody* has duties?"

The Chief laughed. "Well, let's see. I have the over-all headache, and to make up for it I give the orders."

"Orders?" Walt and Orie and John all said.

"It has an ugly sound," said Snarkey, who looked as though he was going to be ready with a sharp remark at every moment of every day.

"I know it has an ugly sound," the Chief admitted. "But any such expedition as ours can exist only if it is a disciplined one, with everybody abiding by the decisions of one leader. I think you know that's true."

Every head nodded solemnly.

"And I might as well start the orders now. First

things first, and the first and last thing I want you all to remember is this: I will insist on careful handling of our equipment and supplies. We're going into a country where lost or damaged gear or provisions cannot be replaced. *Cannot*. And second, we have to keep to schedule. If we don't we'll be stranded without sufficient food before the end of the trip."

"Things could happen," said Mike; he was small, but he looked as if he could manage to weather whatever might happen.

"Don't be afraid, Runt," Franklin chuckled. "The Chief will take care of you."

"We'll all take care of each other," the Chief amended. "The team won't work if one man defaults. Remember that. Just one man. Sure, things happen; but we keep to schedule just the same. If we're stormbound or windbound, we put in extra long days to make up for it. We do the same to balance the time we'll take out for our botanists to work on their collection." He turned to John and Orie. "I hope you're not worrying about time. You'll be given plenty of it in those areas that need particularly detailed research."

The scientists nodded their thanks. "And we'll put in plenty of our own time while the rest of you are fishing!" John added.

At the mention of fishing, Steve's eyes lit up. "I hope you're going to enjoy this as much as we are, Chief." He looked ready to bend his back to a paddle on the instant.

"I always do. It's my life. And more than the accomplishment of the trip itself, I like the things called the intangibles. Like getting the rest of you to understand and love what I do—nature in its original state. The way it was in the beginning. Getting you to understand the importance of making sure some of it stays that way, forever."

He grinned at us all. He is a big man, and his grin is like all outdoors. "I hope you don't mind my lecturing. I always get on a stump when I start talking about the wilderness."

We piled off the *Keenora* at Warren's Landing, at the north end of Lake Winnipeg, and took the launch *Chickama* up the Nelson River to Norway House— a bustling settlement that is one of the lifelines of the fur trade, as are all of the some two hundred Hudson's Bay Company posts. The whole history of Canada centers about the fur trade; the Company itself has little history apart from the country's; and the trapper of today still brings his pelts to the posts to exchange them for salt, tea, sugar, flour, tobacco, fish nets, rifles and knives. The "factories"—York Factory on Hudson Bay, Moose Factory on James Bay, and others—are the main supply depots; early Company agents in charge were called factors. The "houses" are district headquarters.

Norway House was the perfect jumping-off place for our expedition. Our supplies had been ordered from them and were waiting there. After we had reported our proposed route and date of return to the settlement's Mounted Police officer—just to be on the safe side—we headed for the red-roofed white buildings of the Hudson's Bay Company.

The crew whistled at sight of our pile of supplies. Someone exclaimed, "My *gosh!*"

"Wait till you carry it on your back!" laughed Chuck.

It was a mountain—6 feet high, 4 feet wide, and 12 feet long—awesome to behold.

"No one can find room for all that freight and twelve people in just three canoes!" declared Steve. "I don't believe it."

The food was packed in wood boxes, which varied in size and shape but averaged around 12 x 15 x 20 inches. There were 29 of them. Our inventory and check list gave their total weight as 2,131 pounds. Over a ton of food! In addition there were the 12 personal packs of sleeping bags, clothing and other effects averaging 35 pounds each for a total of 420 pounds. The tents, cook kit, chuck box, guns, tackle boxes and miscellaneous items came to 250 pounds. Photographic and scientific equipment added another 250 pounds. The three chestnut freight canoes weighed 160 pounds each. Our staggering total was 3,531 pounds; over a ton and a half. Dry, that is! Drenching rains would make it a great deal heavier. And wet or dry, the three loaded canoes must be emptied and beached every evening, reloaded every morning, and the whole carried over portages en route. This is no country for weak backs.

2

Into the North

STACKED AND STOWED, THE PILES OF GEAR RODE TOO high above the gunwales to present a picture of good canoemanship. But it would have to be that way until we had a chance to cut it down by sorting and repacking. We couldn't afford to leave anything behind. Temporarily, until tests showed where each man could be used to best advantage, Ben was taking the stern and John the bow of the *Chief,* the lead canoe. Chuck and Franklin were to handle the *Shekel,* and Walt and Art the *Esox.*

There are no seats in a freighter. The stern man sits poised on the back plate. The bowman and the two middlemen make perches for themselves on the dunnage with an all-too-small hole left for their feet. It is just an unfortunate coincidence if your paddling position lands you in a section with one sharp-edged wood box under you and another jabbing you in the shins.

Just as we were ready to dip the paddles, some threatening clouds overhead let loose; and before paddling arms were well limbered, the rain turned into a storm. We were crossing Playgreen Lake, a widening of the Nelson River, when from out of nowhere a high wind hit. Rolling waves became higher, white-capped and choppy. An empty canoe would ride them like a cork, but loaded as we were, there was not enough buoyancy. Too far from the mainland, we headed for the nearest island. Pushing hard with a few grunts thrown in, we made slow progress, and some of our greenhorns looked a little startled when waves sloshed over the sides. There was nothing to do but tie up in the lee of the tiny island and wait. It was scarcely an island—more a rock pile with a little scrub timber. There was not enough room to pitch a tent or spread sleeping bags. Imaginations began to run a little wild.

"What if we should be stranded here for days?" one of the boys exclaimed.

There was a snort of laughter from Franklin and Chuck.

"Now that's fanciful dramatizing for you! Why, son, we're still almost within sight of Norway House! We could put our feet on dry land if we had to, and we've got enough food to last for months!"

The storm was one of those swishy, short-lived ones. We pushed the rest of the way across the lake and on to Hope Island. Setting up camp for the first time was a slow, awkward procedure, what with the cooks having to open too many boxes to sort out ingredients for a meal and the rest of the crew not too expert at their assigned jobs. Mike took a steady ribbing for his ignorance and awkwardness. He was youngest and smallest and therefore easiest to rib. The botanists, with a goal of fifteen hundred plant specimens to aim for, averaging forty-four a day, plunged into their project while tents were being pitched and supper prepared. Steve and Mike offered to help with everything, and poor Mike, in someone's way, was whammed on the back by heavyweight Chuck.

"Attaboy! You've really got the spirit of adventure!"

Mike grinned. "Just give me six weeks. We'll see who knows about the wilderness then!"

It is cruel to be awakened at five-thirty of a chilly morning! The thermometer stood at 48°; the ice had been out only a few weeks. It was still early spring—the last week in June. Shivering and allergic to such early rising, we needed a solid breakfast of prunes, oatmeal, bacon, eggs and coffee to put us in good humor. Camp was broken with anything but speed and efficiency, but it was broken.

"Let's go!" said Steve. "Come on, sluggards, when do we hit the trail?"

His face fell when Ben replied, "After your first lesson in canoemanship."

For more than an hour it was demonstration and practice of strokes; the pry, the sweep, the stroke and rudder. And how to develop pure power.

There is good reason why the Indian of the North can travel much farther and faster than the average white man. Most white men sit up straight on a seat and dip the paddle, swinging their arms around in a rather graceful fashion. It looks nice and is entirely adequate for a leisurely lake or stream outing back home.

The Indian leans forward from the waist with each stroke, bringing back and shoulder muscles into play, providing much more force and impetus. His arms, almost stationary, the outside one quite straight and the inner one slightly bent, appear to be used mostly for holding the paddle, with the wrist motions changing the positions of the blade. He paddles all day with a short, quick, rhythmical stroke. He does not lunge laboriously, churning up the water, but dips silently and seemingly without much effort.

If we were to push ourselves to Hudson Bay and back again and be ready for occasions when, perhaps, our lives would depend on matching brute manpower against water power in the treacherously big rivers and fast currents, now was the time to start adopting this Cree technique. For some members of the crew, using back muscles to paddle was new. They would have to unlearn what they had been taught previously.

During the coaching session I snatched a few minutes to go off by myself looking for birds. At home each spring we watch the great migrations. The stopover is brief as they pass on their way to the northern forests to nest. They had arrived here ahead of us, but the timber growth is so dense and the majority of the feathered creatures so tiny and swift of movement that identification is not easy. You hear them, but where are they? These forests can be maddening to an inveterate bird-watcher.

The mouse-collectors had set out their traps during the night, and had caught three of the white-footed variety. Franklin busied himself preparing the skins while the greenhorns were working on canoemanship. "Those," Chuck cruelly remarked, when he saw the finished mouse skins, "look like the fingers of a rubber glove stuffed with sawdust!" Frank threw one at him.

Our various duties and assignments as a twelve-man team were carefully gone over by the Chief for the second time. Just to make sure we knew! All of us were to swing the paddles eight to ten hours a day. All twelve were to help make and break camp. Two of the boys were to gather and chop wood, two to do the dishes, and two to help the cooks. Everybody was to load and unload, and portage.

"Finally, Marion here is aide-de-camp for us all," the Chief finished. "Keeper of the log, weather notes, temperature and barometer readings, notes on fishing conditions, observations on wild life, and anything else she wants to put down—such as how far we make in a day, and why. She'll plan our menus and give the cooks a hand as needed, and first aid and health problems are hers to take care of." He smiled at me and then back at the crew. "Of course, she *wants* most of all to work directly with the botanists, but I doubt if she can wedge that in!"

The Nelson was placid this first morning out, the air still. The shore line became low and marshy with an occasional rocky point jutting out. From the bulrushes and wild rice came the call of the grebes and the booming, pumping sound of the American bittern to break the silence of the forest. On shore were the red dogwood, the low alder bushes and willow shrubs, the pale green leaves of the poplar and birch. Behind them on higher ground came the dark green spires of the spruce as a backdrop. For several hours we pushed on the paddles with an occasional reminder from the Chief: "Unison! Stroke in unison! Put those back muscles to work! That's the ticket!"

The first test for our relatively green crew came during the afternoon as we neared Sea River Falls. Across its entire width the river drops several feet off a ledge. At one point it swirls around the sides of a rock island. We would land at the island, make the carry and put in again below the falls. The current picked up in speed. The approach was full of nasty rocks. A heavily-loaded freighter does not maneuver easily. The lead canoe out ahead gave the other crews an idea of how their craft would respond and when to

start back-paddling to put breaks on the forward momentum. It was tricky, but they handled it. There
were no crash landings, but a round of self-congratula-
tions among the novices instead.

With a distance of only a few rods to cover, this was
not a portage. In canoe language it was a lift-out or
lift-over. But it took a good many trips and a few
grunts and groans to carry the gear and the canoes up
and over to be reloaded at the bottom of the falls; and
before the job was finished the grunts had turned to
mutterings.

"Why couldn't we have run this rapids? There's a
perfectly good channel over there."

"I'd think a good canoeman would have run it!"

"Yeah, I sure didn't come up here to lug tons of
stuff around just for the fun of it."

Ben turned to the complainers sharply, but he kept
his temper. He loses it when a certain effect is needed;
this situation required reasoning. "Yes, there's a
chute," he said, "and no abrupt drop at the point I
picked. But at the end of it the backwash is so high
and ferocious that a loaded canoe would nose-dive and
swamp. A good canoeman doesn't take unnecessary
risks!"

There were hazards enough even with the lift-over.
Loading below the falls in fast water and off a sheer
drop was a devilish job. Floating one canoe at a time
and bringing it broadside, it took the strength of two
men to hold it off the rocks while the rest of us relayed
dunnage to the loader. We had to be on our toes as

we shoved off in the swirling current, for about a hundred feet beyond the island we could see choppy waves where the two channels met and came together head on. We hit, bounced, and shipped about a bucketful of water. To an ardent canoeman there is fascination in white water. It seems to offer an almost irresistible lure regardless of how old he is at the game. Though he would like to feel himself its master, he knows that he is not. He has respect and awe for its power. For the beginners this first taste of rapids was a thrill.

A short paddle brought us to our camp site. The black flies and mosquitoes were out in swarms to greet us. The saying is that the farther north you go, the worse these insects become. This was just a reminder that we were northward-bound, and a sample of what lay ahead. But a good camper never complains of weather, food or insects! Eaten alive, our crew had a stiff struggle. "I'll swallow my gripes," Snarkey vowed as cheerfully as possible, "if I have to swallow a square yard of black flies along with them!"

Mosquito bites itched and flies crawled and bit inside our socks, behind our ears, inside our shirts, and even took a chunk out of an eyelid now and then; but we were so hungry nothing could keep us from our bread and honey, cocoa and stewed apricots.

By the third day on the trail we were gradually getting our ton of food sorted and repacked. A sturdy waterproof chuck box, 26 inches long, 15 inches wide and 22 inches deep, was stocked with staples that are used daily. Muslin bags, labeled with a marking pencil, held such items as salt and pepper, flour, sugar, tea, coffee and oatmeal. Room was reserved for whatever was needed for lunch. One section held the cook kit. Supplies that must be kept dry, such as the hundred pounds each of flour and sugar, were stored in waterproof canvas bags 36 inches long and 18 inches wide.

If it were not for a checking system we would be in a constant state of confusion, opening and pawing through wood boxes searching for needed items. The boxes are numbered. A master list shows the kinds and amounts of food in each. Box number ten, for example, has 36 pounds of macaroni, 24 pounds of rice, 24 pounds of candy bars, 24 pounds of salt and 5 pounds of powdered eggs. There are spaces on the master list for checking off amounts as used. We can see at a glance, for instance, how much butter has been consumed per week. If this has exceeded the quota, it means cutting down the ration.

Canned goods, because of weight, are limited to butter, jam, honey, bacon and powdered milk. There are no canned fruits or vegetables. These are carried in dehydrated form. Even so we are not traveling light, for we have found from past experience that a few so-called luxuries are well worth the extra weight and bulk. If it were not for a limited amount of canned meats there would be nothing but bacon and fish for eight weeks. Eggs, 60 dozen of them, carried in a crate, are bulky but not heavy. If protected and kept cool they keep for many weeks. A hundred pounds of potatoes and a few loaves of bread complete the luxury list. While they last they will provide a more appetizing diet and make it easier for the cooks to prepare meals.

This wood box method of carrying food came in for a bit of criticism from some members of the crew. They had been on short canoe trips and were accustomed to the use of the packsack with shoulder straps, but the advantages of the box would become apparent as time went on.

The packsack is not constructed to carry such heavy weights. Because of size and shape, boxes stack solidly in the canoe without loss of space. They withstand punishment of rough and frequent handling for weeks on end. The food is not mashed to bits by having weight thrown on top of it. And the combination of the wood box, the canvas bag, and the tumpline is the most practical way of packing big loads across the portages. This system was devised early in the days of the fur trade and is still used by the packers of the Hudson's Bay Company.

"Tumpline?" questioned Mike. "What——"

"You'll see!" chortled Franklin, and Chuck rubbed it in.

"Oh, just wait till you see! You'll wish you were home, Runt, you'll wish you were home."

Ten minutes was all that we could pare off the three hours it had taken us yesterday to be ready to shove off. Getting the loaded canoes in motion is rather like starting a freight train in any case, and this morning sore muscles were protesting, adding to the struggle. Until we get under way it always feels as though we are pushing through thick syrup instead of water.

Dozens of swallows, terns and herring gulls wheeled and circled over us as we paddled on down the Nelson. A mother golden-eye duck and fifteen young ones were swimming just ahead of us as we rounded a bend. One of the ducklings was taken for a specimen. Our big find of the day came when we went ashore for our mid-morning stretch and rest. The botanists discovered their first orchid.

By noon a light rain was falling. We were damp and chilled and glad to stop to "boil the kettle"—an expression used in the North for building a fire and having cup after cup of steaming hot tea. Art cooked up a few gallons of soup, using a dehydrated vegetable mix. The directions indicated that the amount he used would make eighty servings, but our gang of twelve polished it off without effort. While we waited for lunch, Ben gave the boys a lesson in preparing bird skins to preserve them and keep them in good condition. We had just shot a sandpiper for the University of Iowa museum, and with it Ben showed the technique of skinning, scraping away flesh and fat, salting, and packing carefully so that feathers are not bent or broken.

The afternoon brought a long hard push through Hairy Lake. Unlike the typical deep, clear-watered lakes of the North, this one is very shallow and choked with water plants. Although the shores are of solid granite rock, the lake itself resembles slough country, the bottom gradually filling in with decaying vegetation. By following devious narrow channels kept open by the current, we were able to struggle through. The two-foot-high bulrushes and reeds got tangled in our paddles, offered a certain amount of resistance and definitely obstructed the view.

Camp was at the far end of this shallow swampy lake. The menu for supper was boiled navy beans, with bacon and onions thrown in for flavor, potatoes, bread and cocoa. There were no dainty, fussy eaters in this crowd, but Franklin ran off with the honors. "Piggy Dunbaugh," the boys called him; and somebody thought up a way to measure his capacity!

The kettle of beans was to be divided in two. Franklin was to be given half, or what was intended for six men, and the rest of us would share the other half. His portion amounted to a few quarts. When he had heaped a pie tin until there wasn't room for another bean, emptied it and repeated the procedure three times, I called a halt to the contest and declared him the champion.

"Ah, Mrs. Ferrier, that's mean! Let him eat. We want to *see!*"

But the Chief took my side. "We can't afford to have one of our key stern paddlers out of commission! Frank is positively the champion, and no more beans tonight!"

The sunset over the lake was spectacular; both sky and water were ablaze. The peace and quiet of the wilderness that often seems accentuated at sunset did not surround us that evening. Hundreds of grebes, terns, gulls, yellow-legs and ducks were all screaming and quacking at once. It sounded like a menagerie. Here was a fine chance for identifying ducks—mallards, American golden-eye, lesser scaup, buffle-head, hooded merganser. We picked up another specimen for the museum—a male horned grebe.

Mike and Steve and Snarkey tried their luck at fishing, and caught several northern pike and a few wall-eyes, including a ten-pound northern. Chuck and Franklin set out their traps. John and Orie went plant-hunting as usual; and I took the evening barometer reading which helps us predict oncoming storms and prepare for them—an important part of wilderness survival.

Only a few days of dishwashing had brought so many pained expressions and gripes over the chore that I had outlined what seemed a simple routine. "Put two kettles of water on the campfire to heat, one for washing and one for rinsing. Collect everything to be washed in one pile. Scrape and stack. Put kettles and skillets to soak. Burn all garbage, flatten and bury tin cans, and leave camp so there is no evidence of our having been here except for the ashes."

I thought that was simple, but every day the dishwashers forgot to put water on to heat until the campfire was nearly out, or failed to scrape and stack and therefore had to wander all over camp, picking up and washing one piece at a time. Or they stuck a greasy frying pan in the clean water first and washed cups and plates later. Or they finally finished, only to have a check show one plate and one spoon missing. That meant a search and delay in breaking camp. Our rules are few, but counting of utensils after each meal is a necessity. They can't be replaced.

As we were loading our gear, an Indian train wound around a bend and past camp. An outboard motor on a lead canoe furnished the power for towing seven loaded freighters. In this land of no roads and no railroads the "canoe brigade" is the only surface means of transporting supplies, and represents in a way the early history of Canada. Over these same routes and by canoe came the explorers and the fur traders hundreds of years ago. Later, by canoe brigade from York Factory, the first settlers worked their way into the interior and on to the west. The only discordant note today was the outboard motor. The Indian has gone modern.

3

Tumpline Torture

We were leaving the great Nelson River to veer off to the northeast, the general direction we were to follow to the Bay.

The waters of the Nelson are rather turbid, for they contain sediment carried all the way from the prairie provinces. But as we entered the Echimamich River, we came into the clean, clear water that typifies nearly all of the streams and the tens of thousands of lakes that extend all the way from our boundary to the Arctic. This vast granite rock area begins around Duluth, Minnesota, fanning out until it stretches over northern Canada from the Mackenzie River in the west across Labrador in the east. This is what the geologists term Pre-Cambrian rock, the oldest in geological history; the original crust of the earth. They state its age not in thousands but in millions of years.

25

During the Ice Age, mammoth glaciers formed. As they moved south, they scraped the earth clean, pushing ahead of them all the soil and depositing it in the agricultural area of middlewestern United States. They left basic rock exposed and gouged out the basins and valleys which were to fill with water and become this maze of rivers and lakes.

Except for an occasional glacial drift of sand, clay and gravel, there is no soil. The only ground cover is duff, the accumulation of decaying vegetation. Over the duff lies a carpet of springy moss. With no soil there are no mud banks, no mud-bottomed waterways. With clean rock shores and rock beds, we get our drinking water by dipping into the lakes and streams with every assurance that it is clean and pure. This is wonderful country. No polluted, contaminated water. No poisonous plants. No poisonous insects. No poisonous snakes. And nature undisturbed and beautiful.

Ben looked ready to deliver one of his favorite speeches, one that says, "The story of civilization is one of destruction of nature." I caught his eye. "Lectures later, Chief! Let them get the feel of nature first. Let them get to know it this way, and they'll understand you better!"

Suddenly, as we rounded a bend in the river, we came face to face with a picture of utter desolation. There was no forest. On both sides and for miles ahead a ravaging fire had left only skeletal reminders of what had once been trees. It was a gruesome sight. It gave us the feeling of being surrounded by death.

Ben said, *"That's* why I'm such a crank about fire." There was no need to remind the crew; their faces told us that. Now they realized, if they hadn't before, why matches are never discarded until they are held by the ends and broken in two; why cigarettes must not only be stamped out but the butts picked up and rolled in a tight wad with the ends of the fingers. Burned fingers will heal. This is why campfires are to be built out on the rocks and near the water, a bucket of water kept handy and sparks watched whenever there is wind; why our fires must not only be wet down but turned over and over and wet down again to make sure there are no hidden embers. This is why we have been warned of the dangers of building a fire near moss. With not a sign of flame or smoke after it has been put out, it may flare up hours later and several feet away where it has crept underground in all directions like fingers. Up here there are no fire rangers, no look-out towers, no fire-fighters to muster, no fancy equipment for controlling or halting a blaze once started.

Echimamich is an Indian word. It means "where two streams come together" or "where water flows both ways." At this lower end of the river, which empties into the Nelson, we were bucking the current. Ahead was the divide. By mid-morning we had come to what is known as the first dam, where the river is no more than fifty to seventy feet wide. In the early days of the fur trade small dams were constructed to raise the water level, eliminating rapids and making the river passable for the thirty-foot York boats. Some of the dams were rebuilt during the nineteen-thirties when the waterways were arterials in developing the gold mines in the interior of northern Canada. Crudely built with upright logs, and behind them a log crib filled with rocks, they served the purpose. This one had seen better days, and appeared to be useless.

The Indians of the canoe brigade we had seen must have camped here at the dam last night. There were feathers and bones about, which indicated a feast of boiled loon and moose, and attached to a moose bone was a sign written in Cree—intriguing and mysterious.

The shore lines now were low with dense willow and alder bushes crowding the banks, the only timber a scattering of jack-pine, lace-curtained tamarack and a few ash. One lone rocky point gave us a place high and dry enough to land for lunch. With freshly-caught northern pike, we made up a sizable kettle of fish chowder. Like many trail dishes, chowder is not made from a recipe. It is concocted from whatever you have.

The river had narrowed down and was too twisting for fast progress, and cold rain had set in. We came to a rocky impassable stretch that required unloading for a lift-over, and then and there decided to camp at the spot. It was a traveler's thoroughfare, but there were not likely to be many travelers coming through, and we had come twenty miles today. We were tired and miserably chilled. We ate supper standing around a

spitting fire in a downpour, raindrops pelting on our
tin plates and making the food soggy and unpalatable.
Water ran up our sleeves and down our necks. We
were drenched to the skin and shivering; by seven-
thirty we had crawled into sleeping bags for the night.

Half an hour later a party of travelers came across
the lift-over and had to make its way around us! Two
white women and a child of about eight—all in
dresses—and a man; a Mennonite missionary and his
family on their way to Winnipeg. It made my teeth
chatter to look at the wind whipping the women's
skirts. Why would anyone go traveling around here
dressed as they were? And then it occurred to me that
I have never seen the native women, Indian or white,
in jeans or slacks. Why they don't freeze or get chewed
to bits by insects, I cannot figure out.

By the fifth day our outfit was beginning to move a
trifle faster in breaking camp. In fact we were quite
proud of ourselves until the morning light revealed
a rip in the canvas of the *Esox*. Ben blew up.

"All right, you men! What did this? Come on, come
on! Something did it! Give out!"

He almost had to pry it out of them.

Yesterday in a bad stretch the *Esox* had hit a rock.
Art, Walt, and Fred had jumped out, but Mike had
not.

"Why not?"

Mike muttered, "The water looked too deep and too
cold!"

Part of what the Chief had to say then was not
printable. The rest of it wasn't new; we heard it every
day; but now it meant more.

*Keep those canoes off the rocks—keep those canoes
off the rocks—keep those canoes off the rocks!* Those
words have been repeated so often they should haunt
us in our dreams. The bowman must be constantly on
the alert for what lies ahead. If you accidentally land
on a rock everyone must jump out. Every man, and
that means *you!* You don't just sit there and try to
shove 'er off. Whenever you come in for a landing
bow first, the front man must jump and break the im-
pact. If brought in parallel, one man jumps out and,
from a sitting position, holds the canoe off shore by
grasping the gunwales with both hands and extending
his feet to act as a cushion. On occasions when we go
ashore without unloading, the bow may be lifted
out on smooth rock or a pole slipped underneath so
the craft can be rolled. It is never to be left before it
is tied to a tree with a round turn and two half hitches.
When beached for the night the canoe is carried back
some distance from shore, turned bottom side up, and
tied securely.

The upper Echimamich kept getting more and more
narrow and so twisting and tortuous that many times
we could not get the big freighters around corners
without backing up and making another try. Meanwhile we were ducking under overhanging alder and
willow branches, getting well switched. Sometimes we
threw windfalls over the rocks and lifted the loaded

canoes up and over. It was slow going—about two miles an hour. The only compensation was that with the shrubs and trees so near, we could see the birds at close range: Canada jays, cedar waxwings, red-eyed vireo, red-tailed hawks, spotted sandpipers. Around each bend we put ducks to flight. The botanists spied and collected their second orchid.

Lunch time brought us to the second dam which was put in to raise the water level in a divide lake which lay ahead. The divide is the source of two rivers, the Echimamich, flowing west, and the Hayes to the east. The dam helps to keep the lake high enough for the water to flow in both directions.

Our first long portage was coming up. "Tell 'em how the Indians do it, Chief," urged Franklin and Chuck. "They won't believe anything *we* say."

"Well," Ben told the others, "it's the tumpline that makes it possible to carry tremendous loads. The Indian literally grows up with a tumpline. By the age of five or six, a child can portage 20 to 30 pounds. The white man who is able to carry a load equal to his own weight considers himself a tower of strength. Yet it is not unusual to see a short, thin, emaciated 135-pound Cree come along with two boxes and two sacks of flour weighing 320 pounds; and women have been known to carry over 200 pounds. With the tumpline the main bulk of the weight comes on top of the head.

"When a canoe brigade starts off on a long freighting haul to a distant post, instead of making it grueling, disagreeable labor, the Indian crew turns it into a contest. A game. At the end they boast. Who broke camp the fastest? Who carried the most? Who broke the record for the distance covered in a day? They do not walk over a portage. They dog-trot. Possibly they figure that if they run they get the agony over with that much faster!"

Franklin and Chuck roared at the look on Mike's face when Ben said that.

The white man who can equal or surpass the Indian when it comes to packing is an exception. Ben had met one many years ago in the Berens River country—a trapper. Of Slavic origin, Joe Radyk stood over six feet and weighed around two hundred pounds. "I was awestruck," Ben told us. "That hulk of a man lifted an immense metal trunk from his canoe and walked off with it as though it were a bag of feathers."

The tales that the natives told about Joe Radyk seemed almost legendary. Joe could walk a mile with a load of 400 pounds without putting it down. Starting off alone in his canoe with 1,000 pounds of freight, he could travel 150 miles in three days. He had even been seen to tump together and carry eight 100-pound sacks of flour. Ben had traveled with him once for three days, and from him had learned many tricks of tying, lifting and balancing loads, tricks which we would have a chance to try out at Robinson Portage, just ahead.

Not one of us was feeling like a would-be Goliath. Nearly everyone was suffering from aching arms and shoulders. I dug out and passed around analgesic balm for massages, and everyone worked on those complaining muscles. Robinson Portage was tough. A cold driving rain had kept us in a state of soppy chill all day. We crossed our fingers and hoped for clearing weather; the barometer was on the way up.

We got our wish. July 1 brought hot, bright sunshine, and a chance to spread our wet dunnage over half an acre to dry. Two Indian families, men, women, children, and some roly-poly sled-dog puppies, were making the fifty-foot carry over Painted Stone Portage. They were on their way to Norway House, and no doubt would cover the distance much faster than we had, for the natives are hard travelers. It is the rule rather than the exception that when they hit the trail, they keep going around the clock with only a few hours of rest for days at a time, if necessary, to reach their goal. We had more than a slight suspicion that they were putting on a show for the strange white men; they ran back and forth tossing their equipment carelessly, chattering in Cree and giggling like children.

Before we had been paddling very long that morning, we were over the divide and in the Hayes River. It was marshy country; there was no place to land for lunch. We ate candy bars instead, to give us energy enough to keep the paddles swinging.

The landscape changed back to hills of massive granite as we came to Robinson Lake. An eight-mile stretch of open water to cross is a challenge to the canoeman, but with favorable weather, we felt no qualms. Then, when we were no more than halfway across, from out of nowhere the wind suddenly shifted, came straight at us with the force of a small gale. The heavens opened up for a downpour, and the battle was on. Drenched again! With Robinson Portage ahead of us: a long five-sixths of a mile. It was tough enough having it come before toting muscles were hardened and before we had consumed much of that ton of food. To pack almost a mile what had started out to be 3,500 pounds was a man-killer in itself before adding nobody knew how much weight in rain water.

It was late afternoon by the time we put our feet on shore. Dripping, forlorn and fagged out from battling the waves, the rain and a head wind, this should have been the end of the day. We had already been on the trail and working hard for eight hours. But we were just getting started. Wearily we unloaded, stacking the wood boxes in one pile, the packsacks in another, canvas bags and tents in a third, and miscellaneous articles in a fourth. Paddles were taken off the path and placed against a tree so they wouldn't be stepped on. Waterproof tarps were thrown over the dunnage to keep things from getting wetter.

"It's a nice gesture, anyway," said Snarkey. "But can they get any wetter?"

"Hey, look, there's a teaser!" called Steve. He had spotted the vestiges of rails and a flat-topped pushcar built many years before to make it easier for those going over a well-traveled route—when it was one.

Now the rails were rusted, the ties rotted out, and the car had fallen apart. Teaser was right.

An advance guard of mosquitoes and black flies met us, followed shortly by the whole army, thousands of them. Repellents dabbed on exposed faces and hands seemed to be just an invitation to the tormentors to show us all the spots we had missed. Nothing short of a bath in the stuff would have been effective. With the job that faced us, there was no time to stand around fussing about insects.

During the past week Ben had been sizing up the crew and, by now, had a good idea of how to distribute the loads according to age, muscular development and experience. The youngest and least experienced would start out with 75 to 100 pounds. Later this could be increased. The older boys would take up to 125 pounds, and the huskier men 125 to 200 pounds. This first portage would take at least four trips. That meant crossing seven times for a total distance of about six miles. Three and a half of those miles would be trudged burdened with a heavy load.

"O.K., greenhorns!" shouted Franklin cheerily. "There's a mountain to be moved! Let's see you show the Chief how much you can carry."

The crew took it grinning, but half-seriously. This was their initiation into the use of the tumpline. The 16-foot leather strap, with tapered thongs attached to a 3-inch-wide headband, is indispensable for carrying heavy loads. Invented by the early fur traders, it is still universally used in the far North.

The technique was demonstrated on Steve. The two thongs strapped around the ends of a box were each tied with a canoe knot—a simple slip knot with the end doubled over as it came through the loop. A pull on the long end of the thong tightens it. A tug at the short end unties it. The box was now raised high enough on Steve's back so that he could slip the headband in position on his forehead. With the slack released, the box came to rest over the lower back. Then, while he bent forward from the hips and put his hands on his knees for a brace, Ben lifted a canvas food sack and let it down on top of this box platform. As Steve straightened up, almost the entire weight was borne on his head. To offset the terrific backward pull on his neck, a second bag was hoisted on top of the head lengthwise and extending out beyond the forehead. He looked a bit solemn and unhappy as he started plodding across the portage, but he took it as he took anything dished out to him, without comment or complaint. He even managed a feeble salute when Frank and Chuck called after him, "See you there sometime tonight!"

When it comes to portaging, my size and sex put me at the bottom of the list. I am not even allowed to use a tumpline. "You're not getting out of this, though, Marion," Ben said. "There's always the miscellaneous pile. You can take some of that little light stuff."

I sorted out what seemed a small share compared to what the others were carrying. To keep from being eaten alive, I rigged myself in a heavy jacket, gloves, and head-net. Pants cuffs were tucked inside long wool socks, for I knew that repellents would be useless unless someone followed me with a spray gun. It took some maneuvering to find a way to carry the collection I had settled on. The rucksack on my back weighed 35 pounds. The Graflex camera, housed in a specially made sturdy wood box and weighing 15 pounds, was slung over one shoulder and bounced off my left hip. A motion picture camera, 15 pounds, did the same on my right hip. In each hand I carried an iron box filled with our precious film—20 pounds. Since the front of me was still unencumbered, I hung two small knapsacks with the straps over the back of my neck so they could bounce along on my abdomen just for the ride. The whole came to over 85 pounds. Just the little light stuff!

The going wasn't too tough at first as I struggled up a long incline and on down into a low marshy stretch. Then things started happening. Those pesky little black flies were finding some hole and crawling inside my head-net. They were biting my eyelids and inside my ears. Gaps had developed between my gloves and shirt sleeves. My socks were down. Mosquitoes by the dozens were feasting on wrists and ankles. With both hands full, there was no way to swat or shoo. The two camera boxes were giving my hip bones a crack with each step. The straps of the rucksack began cutting into my shoulders. The weight of the iron boxes was making my fingers ache. The trail was wet and slippery, a combination of moss-covered rocks, holes and mud. The rusted ten-inch spikes protruding at crazy angles from the rotting railroad ties were a hazard to moccasined feet. And those feet were refusing to track straight. I tried stepping from one rail tie to the next but more often than not I slid off or missed them entirely, coming down so hard that I was jarred to the teeth.

Perspiring and aching all over, I stepped off the trail, dropped the two iron boxes, and eased the weight of the rucksack by leaning against a windfall. I was afraid that if I sat down I wouldn't be able to get up again. To make it the rest of the way, I would have to put mind over matter. Perhaps by concentrating hard on counting paces I could forget the misery. It took me awhile to figure out how many yards there would be in five-sixths of a mile and about how many steps that would be. I decided that surely, by now, I had covered half the distance. If I could hold out long enough to plunk one foot in front of the other seven hundred and fifty times, I'd have it licked.

Back on the trail. One hundred steps. Two hundred. There was more light now coming through the dense forest. Another hundred paces and I could catch a glimpse of blue water ahead. All that was left was to negotiate a steep hill down to a rock ledge and the shore of the river.

It had taken me an hour to walk less than a mile. As the rest of the crew came staggering down that last hill, they were a sorrowful looking lot. Walt's boxes had been riding too high and had rubbed the skin off along his spine. Snarkey's whole load had started slipping to one side. Tired as we were we found we could still laugh as we watched him come into camp on a slant. Mike had lost one bag altogether and had to go back after it.

I didn't need to ask them how they felt. They were expressing their opinions in no uncertain terms. Some of the language they wouldn't use in front of their mothers!

"I feel like somebody'd been applying a full Nelson on me all the way across. Driving my chin clear into my chest!" declared Frank.

"You're wrong," John said. "It's a series of sledge-hammer blows on the top of your head."

"It's a fifty-pound piece of lead fastened to each foot," groaned Fred, rubbing his legs. His thighs pained, not from the load on his back, but just from trying to lift his feet off the ground.

And Steve swore he must be two inches shorter from having his head telescope into his neck.

Without the tumpline, freighting of tons of supplies would be next to impossible, but if its inventor had appeared at that moment, he would have been annihilated.

4

Canoe Practice

WHEN BEN CAME STAGGERING IN UNDER A 200-POUND load, he was bombarded with complaints—and then he had to boost morale enough to get them all going for a second trip. After that, we stopped for supper, in order to get up strength for a third load. It was almost midnight before the last man limped again into camp. Eight hours of paddling and eight hours of portaging. Quite a day. And there were still the three canoes and a few odds and ends. It is possible for a man to portage one of these freighters alone, but it is a feat left for the experienced packer. It is too heavy to carry on his shoulders with a yoke. He must use the tumpline with the weight resting on his head and neck. Even the method we use, the two-man carry, is a tough assignment. Our crew was allowed to wait until morning to tackle it.

There are four main thwarts. While two men lift the bow, the front man, with shoulders well-padded with jackets or sweaters, crawls into position where paddles have been tied to the two front thwarts leaving room for his head in between the blades. The stern man then lifts the back end. With the gunwales on his shoulders and the back of his neck against the stern plate, he extends his arms forward to grasp the sides for balance. The bowman bears the greatest burden of weight. It is a back-breaking job for both of them, and since the canoe is twenty inches deep, it is like trying to walk with a big wood box over your head, and the box, incidentally, filled with mosquitoes and black flies. There are no hands free to shoo or swat. All you can do is curse. Vision is limited to your two plodding feet and a very short distance ahead. You hope and pray there is not another party coming along with a canoe from the opposite direction.

By nine-thirty the last canoe was over. We were loaded and ready to shove off down the Hayes River. The shore line was low and marshy with a luxuriant growth of cattails, bulrushes, pickerel weed and elodea. Black terns by the dozen were hovering and darting over us in agitation. Nesting time—and they resent the intrusion. There were juncos, golden-crowned kinglets, Canada jays, a pileated woodpecker. As we rounded one bend we heard a most familiar song, and there, sure enough, was a fat cock robin, surely one of the more adventuresome of his kind.

With twelve people there are not many intervals in the day when the peace of the wilderness is not broken by the sound of human voices. Usually it is confined to reasonable conversational tones. But about the time the crew of the *Shekel* decides to communicate their thoughts to a buddy in the *Esox* or the *Chief* there is enough noise to frighten the wildlife for miles around. It might be that we were too tired to talk after yesterday's grind. At any rate during one of those rare interludes when there was not a sound except for the swish of the paddles, our approach was evidently unheralded. There, perhaps fifty yards ahead of us, was a majestic bull moose feeding in the river.

Had we planned it that way, the timing could not have been more perfect. Before he saw us or smelled us, the huge head and antlers arced down as he submerged for another mouthful of lily tubers. Now only a great dark brown hump was visible. Out came the cameras. While he was still preoccupied with foraging for his breakfast we paddled hard to get as close as possible. Then as the great horns and his nose came to the surface, we froze. There he was, in full view, munching away, his antlers festooned with dripping water plants. Suddenly he stopped chewing—the nose lifted—he turned and stared at us for perhaps ten seconds. Cameras clicked and whirred. Then he wheeled, lunged for shore and disappeared into the dense growth of spruce.

To come upon game unexpectedly and get close enough for a good shot is a wildlife photographer's dream. Usually it takes endless patience and effort; patient waiting in mosquito-infested holes, and effort to set the stage just right. A full-grown bull stands as much as six feet high to the shoulder, weighs up to fifteen hundred pounds, and his great palmated antlers may have a six-foot spread. It is not difficult to spot an animal that is larger than a horse. But to be able to approach for a close-up without his being aware of your presence, to get into position where the lighting is right, to jockey around so that once he sees or smells you, he will be cut off and cannot make a dash for shore, takes a combination of strategy and hard work with a little luck thrown in. You want something more recorded on film than a rear view or an indistinct blob of his dark brown coat blended into the dark green backdrop of the spruce forest.

If the wind is coming in your direction instead of toward him, you may be able to paddle to within ten or fifteen yards of a moose before he shows any alarm; his sense of smell is much keener than his eyesight or hearing. If you have been able to get between him and the shore, his only recourse for escape is to swim out across the lake or river. In spite of his great bulk and weight he is such a good swimmer that men must use every ounce of strength to keep up with him.

"If you don't wear out before he does," Ben told our crew, "you can come up alongside so close that it would be possible to leap from the canoe onto his back. I've done it—grabbed the horns and gone for a ride. But you'd better be off before his feet touch bot-

tom if you don't want to be carried into the forest
and hung on a limb to dry!"

It is often said that early morning and evening are
the most favorable times for observing moose as they
come to the river or lake to drink and feed, but Ben
has found that they do not keep to schedule. They
appear at any hour of the day. Chances of seeing them
boil down to being at the right place at the right time.
Hot, humid weather offers the best bet for catching
them well out away from shore, for they may wade in
up to their necks and stand for long periods to keep
cool and escape the flies and insects.

Somebody mentioned the thrill of shooting a
moose, and Ben snapped, "Most white men have no
motive for killing moose except to brag of their prowess or display the mounted head! Our moose have
been so cut down by slaughter that the season is
closed in most sections now. And a good thing too! A
native kills for meat and fur and hide, and that's a
different matter."

Our would-be hunter said no more.

We left the Hayes River to head off on a more east-
erly course toward God's Lake, which we expected to
reach in another week. A portage over a steep hill
put us into the first of a whole chain of unnamed
lakes. A paddle of only a mile and a half, another and
longer portage, and we camped for the night beside
a small crystal lake surrounded by granite cliffs and
dotted with little wooded islands.

Just as the mountain climber is lured by new peaks

and performs feats of skill and endurance to scale them, so it is with those who seek out nature's marvels in the deep northern forests. To some it would seem, perhaps, that the mountain climber struggles to reach a goal that holds nothing but the other side of the mountain. Or that such enthusiastic canoe cruisers as our party simply make beasts of burden of themselves in order to reach one lake or river after another that are all the same as those they left behind them.

Our crew scoffed at that kind of thinking. There is never a monotony to the out-of-doors. No two mountains, lakes or rivers are alike. Each has its individuality. Besides, there is always the "beyond" that is hard to reach and worth the effort.

From our camp on a high rock point there was a breathtaking view. This was not a big, grand, magnificent lake. Its beauty was on such a small scale that we felt we could drink it in all at once. It might have been its purity that made us suddenly feel very dirty and out of harmony with our surroundings. John, Orie and Chuck shaved for the first time in a week, and Frank washed his face for the first time since we left Norway House!

We built a smudge to drive out the hordes of mosquitoes, and then we sat around watching six beautiful loons put on a show for us. Unlike most other creatures of the wild, loons are not timid. They are company for many a lone traveler. They are there to welcome him to almost every secluded northern lake.

Whether their loud and varied calls are meant as alarm, defiance, curiosity or friendliness, once their territory is selected and claimed for the summer they do not retreat for man or beast.

The six of them at our campsite entertained us for an hour or more as they screamed, yodeled, chased each other around in circles, dove, and played hide-and-seek, stood on their tails, or rolled on their sides and waved their feet.

"Now I know what 'crazy as a loon' means," said Snarkey, his freckled face full of amusement. "They're nuts!"

The Chief gave us a day of rest here, and everyone relaxed except John and Orie. A day in camp couldn't be a holiday for our plant collectors. By the time we reached God's Lake they hoped to have at least five hundred specimens, and that meant work. Meticulous work. It's not how pretty you think a plant is that counts, but its condition when it finally reaches the laboratory and the completeness of the scientific data for each specimen. It was a bit deflating to find that John and Orie had no use for a handful of posies you picked for them or even for a whole plant pulled up by the roots and presented to them in a somewhat mangled, wilted state. We stopped trying to be helpful after awhile and confined ourselves to pointing out new discoveries.

Each one of the hundreds of plants must be carefully dug out with a geologist's or botanist's pick and be complete with root, stems, leaves, and either flower or fruit. As soon as possible the specimens must be deftly arranged between folded blotting sheets, with corrugated cardboard between each layer, and clamped tightly into a plant press. Attached to each specimen is a sheet of accurate notes that give the story of when and where it was found; descriptive colorations; whether it flourished in sand, limestone, clay, peat, or poked its head out of a crack in the granite rock; whether it thrived in the cool darkness of the forest or preferred a sunny open cliff or a marshy shore.

Since the end product must be perfectly dry, each plant has to be carefully transferred to new blotting papers at about twenty-four hour intervals for several days. Eventually they are all stored away in specially constructed boxes with paradichlorobenzene crystals sprinkled in to discourage any accumulation of fungus growth. It is a seemingly endless, tiresome job and our botanists put in long hard hours. As the collection grew, the bulk of our gear that we were able to cut down by consumption of food was replaced by the bulging plant presses.

There was a day when half the crew simply burrowed deeper into their sacks after the rising call. That would have been bad enough, but we had a portage to make before we could go any farther, and they weren't ignorant of the fact. To make an impression he hoped would be lasting, the Chief blew up.

He tore into their tents and practically ripped them one by one from their sleeping bags. And you could have heard him in Winnipeg.

"Make up your minds now!" he roared. "If you want to sleep you can stay where you are for the summer. If you want to go on with the expedition, get up and do the portaging. You've had more rest than some others around here—so you can portage without help. I think that's fair!"

Breakfast was gulped down in silence, and the portaging done in clouds of gloom. But they never failed to rise at the call again.

The Fourth of July was not a holiday for us. We had three portages that day, as we pushed through a string of nameless lakes in a pouring rain. We waded through small rapids, edging through the rocks by tipping the canoes slightly to reduce the width. When the rocks were too near the surface, or the granite floor was too slimy, there was trouble for someone, and finally defeat and a portage.

We got so wet we decided to building a Swampy Cree fire—a fire of Paul Bunyan dimensions which serves three purposes in the North country. First you start a blaze with tinder, sticks and branches. Then six logs of dead wood about eight inches in diameter and ten to twelve feet long are dragged up, placed on end cross-logs and spaced conveniently for holding cook kettles. The flames from the "squaw wood" will start curling and licking through the logs, and before long you have a magnificent fire. There is room for twelve people to huddle and get thawed out and at least partially dry. You have also a man-sized kitchen range; and—not to be sneezed at—the smoke drives out the hordes of mosquitoes and black flies.

Pushing on again in the afternoon, we found we could barely move in a shallow, narrow, tortuous creek. Hairpin turns were too sharp for our nineteen-foot craft, and time and again we had to nose into the opposite bank and back up for another try. Paddles began to hit bottom. Middlemen got out to lighten the loads and fought their way through a swamp; but still the canoes bogged down. Nothing to do but portage again. It was a quarter of a mile, that portage, and it took two and a half hours to make.

Later, we were in a shallow lake full of the muck of decaying vegetation. With our freighters drawing from nine to twelve inches in a depth of no more than eighteen inches, it was like trying to paddle through sorghum molasses—not just the usual starting syrup.

Total length of the day's portages: a mile and an eighth. Back and forth seven times over each one. That came to a total of almost eight miles, and about five miles of that staggering under tumpline loads. When I mentioned this to the crew, there was a round of complaint. "That's bad psychology! Don't *tell* us things like that! It just makes us more tired!"

"Well," I admitted, "maybe it *is* better to try to

forget about distance. Maybe it *would* be better just
to put one foot in front of the other; one foot in front
of the other; one foot——"

Eleven male voices shouted at me to shut up!

The trail was faint through a floating bog on which
a misstep could have put us in up to our necks. We
thought it would be better on a ledge. But a ledge
that narrowed down to a foot in width with a sheer
drop to the fast water below was no more comfortable
than the floating bog. Best going that day was on the
muskeg—that spongy moss-covered ground where the
ice lies two to three feet below the surface and never
entirely melts.

It was becoming more and more obvious that we
were on a seldom-traveled route. In the days when
word got around of the discovery of gold in the God's
Lake area the traffic out of Norway House was heavy.
On the portages corduroy sidewalks had once been
laid in the marshy areas. Occasionally we saw the
rotted remnants of them. Now we sank and waded.
Windfalls across the trail had once been cut out. Now
they were moss-covered, and the down trees lay at
crazy angles to make the going difficult. We had the
choice of going around, over, or under them. Paths
once well-trampled by moccasined feet now tangled
us in dense brush and overhanging branches.

Since the nineteen-thirties the mines of the interior of Canada have been serviced and supplied
mainly by plane and by the winter tractor train. On
this old route and on many others in the Far North,

the wilderness trails that have been by-passed with the introduction of modern transportation are reclaiming themselves. Nature has been using her eraser on the marks of man.

What a Fourth of July! Even after we were fed, the plant collectors could not call it a day and crawl into their tents. The plant presses, full of their precious specimens, were wet along with everything else. It was essential that the plants be kept dry; so essential that John and Orie had brought along with them a one-burner gasoline stove. With a tarpaulin draped over wood boxes and up-ended canoe paddles they fashioned a shelter and set up a drying room. Weary as they were, they worked for hours shifting the presses around to catch the heat from their little stove.

The next day was better going, and in the evening, on another unnamed lake, Ben ordered coaching and practice in canoemanship. Up to now we had been in waters where caution combined with the fundamentals of canoe cruising brought us through safely. The God's River was an entirely different story. We had to be prepared for it, and that required mastering skills far superior to those we had developed so far.

Ever since Norway House the crew had been hearing tales of the treachery and perils of the God's, of how seldom it is traveled and of how, if we met with an accident or disaster, it might be weeks or even months before we could get out or anyone would find us. God's River had become almost like an apparition lying in wait for us.

In these calm, safe waters mistakes could be made without danger. The crew could practice strokes and techniques over and over and over. They could learn how all four men could jump out of the canoe in unison on command, without tipping over, of course. At first they were awkward and if the canoes had been loaded, our precious supplies would have been jeopardized. Before long they could do it without a jiggle.

By the time we started down the God's River they would have to be adept at skulling, snubbing, prying. They would have to master the swing stroke, the fishtail and the cross-bow rudder. By setting up an imaginary figure-eight obstacle course they were able to zig and zag, in and out, around and around, finding out how the canoe would respond to each stroke and when to use it.

Since the bow paddlers assume a key role in fast white water, they came in for an extra amount of drilling. Going at break-neck speed they must be able to swing the bow quickly to the right or left. Often this requires split-second decisions and a powerful pull. The situation here on the lake was make-believe but they could pretend that there were barely submerged jagged rocks looming up directly ahead of them.

On this mill-pond surface it was not possible to get the feel of balance and counterbalance. There are

times when catastrophe can be avoided only by knowing in which direction and how much it is necessary
to lean to bring the canoe back on an even keel when
sudden unexpected currents twist, turn and tilt it
from side to side. Our men were taught what to do
if they were ever caught in the predicament of having a swift current whirl them around in a half circle
so that they found themselves going downstream
backwards. It wouldn't do to have one man quick-
witted enough to swing around and madly paddle
north while his companions were still facing south!
All four must pivot to reverse completely their positions—and this without a side-to-side shift of weight
resulting in a tip-over. Such an acrobatic feat requires
practice.

The intensive coaching session lasted all afternoon,
and the Chief promised more of the same for another
time.

Departure from Walleye Lake the following morning brought an abrupt change of landscape. The high
granite hills receded into the background and for the
next seventy miles or more the route led through a
flat basin with marshy shores, the bays choked with
water plants—reeds, rushes, arum, smartweed and water lilies; the banks a mat of willow, alder, poplar and
jack pine. It was a haven for waterfowl. There were
terns and gulls by the hundreds, and ducks and more
ducks.

At this time of year, when the babies are small, the
lame duck acts put on for us are most entertaining.

Giving the high sign to her young ones to make tracks for shore and hide, the duck then leaves them and performs all sorts of antics in order to focus our attention on her instead of the ducklings. One mallard did an unusually thorough job of it. Flying low, she landed just ahead of our canoe. Then she beat her wings helplessly as though she was crippled and unable to take off. Finally she let her head hang to one side as though she had been shot. Whenever we came a bit too close for comfort she would take off, fly a short distance, and repeat the whole performance. After about ten minutes of this foolishness she wheeled around and returned to her little ones.

With such flat topography there was plenty of room for the water to spread out to form very large and very shallow lakes. Between us and God's Lake, which was now only three travel days away, stretched two formidably large bodies of water; Aswapiswanan, some sixteen miles long, and Touchwood, about twenty-five miles long. Mother Nature would dictate when and how we would cross them, but Ben gave us a briefing on the rules for safe travel.

"On large lakes, stay close to shore. If the shore line is an irregular one with deep bays, cross from point to point only in calm water. If possible, keep land such as islands between you and the open lake. It affords shelter from a direct blow and a lee side to tie up to in case of a storm. If you're caught in a rough sea, head the canoe at quarter angle to the waves. With a tail wind paddle at a good clip. This has a tendency to keep the canoe riding the crests and prevents water washing over the stern. If you must head into the wind, travel slowly so the bow will not plow and ship water."

Aswapiswanan and Touchwood posed special problems not covered by the rules. We were under no illusions that their shallowness made them safe. A large shallow lake can be glassy smooth and then with a sudden wind become a wild choppy sea in a matter of minutes. In the shallows we would have to be constantly on the alert for submerged rocks. In rough water we would be unable to see them. An empty canoe will ride over high rolling waves like a cork, but with our loads we could take no chances of mounting a crest and then coming down with a crash, smack on top of a hunk of granite. Our chief concern was that we had no choice but to strike out over great expanses of open water. At times we would be miles from shore with no protective islands. A crossing without any dangers would depend not only on starting off under favorable conditions but predicting the weather for several hours in advance.

By the time we had made a portage to cut off a loop of the river leading to Aswapiswanan, we were encountering gusty squalls. Then we saw the lake, and it was full of dancing white caps. It might be hours or it might be days before the wind went down enough for us to venture out across that body of water. We had to find a spot high and dry enough to pull in and tie up, but the swampy river banks offered nothing.

Sneaking around the corner and hugging the left-hand shore, we escaped the full force of the gale and headed for what appeared to be a narrow strip of sand beach. As we came nearer we saw some small buildings, a strange sight in this uninhabited land. It was an Indian winter camp. Judging by the number of one-room shacks, we decided it was an encampment for several families for their winter trapping operations. All were of similar size and construction—logs chinked with moss and plastered over with clay. Berry bushes grew on the moss-covered roofs. There were poles extending from tree to tree for hanging and skinning moose and caribou, and poles about five to eight feet off the ground were arranged for spreading fish nets to dry. On the cabin roofs were bones, probably the remains of meat stored there out of reach of the sled dogs. The dogs, too, in this particular camp evidently had shelter, for there were kennels measuring about three by five feet.

Inside, the cabins were all very much alike. In the center of the room stood an old rusty stove. In one corner a platform covered with straw apparently served as a bed for the whole family. Other than this there was no furniture of any kind. The stench was terrific. It would be difficult to imagine what the cabins would be like when occupied.

There was no pretense of any provision for sanitation facilities. If an Indian is living in a tent, he can pick up his home and move to a clean lot when the surroundings become too filthy. But from the white man he has learned to live in houses; these nauseating surroundings, along with a great deal of disease, are the result in the North.

As we waited for the wind to subside we gulped down a lunch of tea and boiled rice and raisins. Mike kept holding his nose in between swallows, and Snarkey prayed volubly for the weather to clear. An hour later we were able to set out across the miles of open water. A favorable tail-wind helped to push us, but we knew that wind can change direction and force in a matter of minutes, and that there is more danger of swamping in a shallow lake than in deep water. We could only hope for the best.

Once launched on Aswapiswanan, there was no place to land until we reached the other side. Hour after hour it was heave and shove, heave and shove without missing a stroke. On a large lake with low shore lines, distances are deceiving. What looks to be one mile is more nearly three or four. Push, push, push. No matter how hard we worked, the far shore seemed to get no closer. Had a half-mile portage suddenly loomed up ahead of us it would have been a welcome sight. At least it would have given us a chance to stretch our legs and use a different set of muscles. Only the realization of impending danger kept us leaning on those paddles until finally we dragged ashore in a horrible mosquito-infested hole of a campsite at the entrance of the Mink River.

A hard ten-hour day had put us thirty miles closer to God's Lake. Backs, necks and arms were aching. Our seats were sore from being perched on those hard wood boxes for hours without being able to move. But Aswapiswanan was behind us. We could have been windbound for days in that filthy Indian camp.

Somebody remarked on the blessing of our deliverance. "I can still smell it," said Mike. "Phew!"

"Piggy" Dunbaugh blithely remarked that *he* wouldn't mind if the rest of us were still too nauseated to eat our supper.

5

Paddle and Portage

THE NEXT MORNING THE BAROMETER WAS VERY HIGH, the temperature was 62°, and the sky had a too-windy look. The Mink River was narrow and it was fast. The dense forest growth of alders, spruce, jack pine, and now and then a tamarack, seemed to be crowding in on us from both sides. The banks came closer and closer together and the water, confined into smaller and smaller space, picked up speed. There were rapids ahead. We heard them before we saw them, and then as we rounded a sharp bend, there was the white water rolling and bouncing, hissing and roaring downhill. The river had narrowed from one hundred and fifty to twenty feet.

We made a landing to study it from shore. There seemed to be plenty of water. A loaded canoe cannot be taken through if there is a sheer drop of even a foot, for the bow would nose into the backwash, but here there seemed to be a safe smooth-rolling chute. The only catch was that the chute rolled between two juicy rocks so close together that there would be only about one foot of clearance on each side of the canoe. That spot would have to be hit right on the nose and our big freighters were not too maneuverable. Here, as in most rapids, the canoe would have to be moving faster than the current, and that would be plenty fast. Should it come into the white water too slowly it would be out of control and at the mercy of the currents.

This rapids could be run but it was too tricky for the skills developed thus far by most of our crew. They were disappointed when they learned that this would be a demonstration, with most of us watching how it was done. The Chief chose Franklin as his bowman. The rest of us picked good vantage points on shore. We saw them put in up above the bend and come arcing around, paddling like mad to get up speed before they hit the white water. Just as they approached the chute Franklin reached forward with his long arms in a powerful bow rudder to pull the front end into position. Ben paddled hard on the opposite side to increase the forward motion and at the same time, by quick rudder strokes, kept the stern from swinging. They swooshed right through the center of the chute between those two rocks—with a thousand pounds of freight! Beaching the first canoe beyond

the fast water, they repeated the performance twice
to bring the other canoes through.

The rest of the morning was taken up by two portages of one-eighth and three-eighths of a mile around
falls and rapids. As we neared the mouth of the Mink
River and saw the wide expanse of Touchwood spreading out ahead of us, whitecaps told us that we were
windbound again.

The boys were itching to reach God's Lake, and
they found it hard to be patient. But a woodsman is
forced to learn patience. Mere man gains nothing by
bucking, battling and stewing when nature interferes
with his plans. The city man eats, works, and travels
by the clock, but time loses significance in primitive
surroundings. The man who spends much of his life
in the bush prepares himself to deal with emergencies
arising out of nature's changing moods. He takes no
unnecessary risks, but resigns himself to abiding by
her dictates with equanimity.

Ben is very positive about this, and he kept at it
with our crew. "The veteran woodsman is rare who
has a fund of stories about his own hair-raising adven-
tures. He knows that if he boasts about a life packed
with danger and near catastrophe it stamps him as
being either inexperienced or stupid. Oh, you may
find one who delights in weaving wonderful tales—
embellished, exaggerated or wholly fabricated—for
the benefit of the tenderfeet from outside. Accidents
can happen to the most experienced, but on the

whole the man who brags about tip-overs or being lost, or nearly starved, or the like, is not a great he-man. He's just green!"

It would have been exciting to head out into those choppy waves with a good chance of crashing down on a rock and caving in the ribs of a canoe or swamping and losing all of our supplies. Anxious as we were to reach God's Lake, we preferred to skip the thrills and find a place to land. Sitting out a blow was not a waste of time.

The botanists, welcoming every hour that they had on shore, put in a full and busy afternoon. One of the most interesting biological aspects of the trip was that, as we pushed north, their collection did not show an advance in season as it would have done if we had stayed in one location. The calendar said it was the second week in July but many of the flowers just coming into bloom were those we are accustomed to seeing in May: violets, anemones, buttercups, cowslips and bunch-berry.

With the wind showing signs of abating, there was an order from the Chief for a quick easy evening meal with as little unpacking of supplies as possible. The cooks chose scrambled eggs as the solution.

As often happens, the wind went down with the sun. The lake became almost glassy. It was too late to cover the more than twenty miles of Touchwood but we would go as far as we could that evening. Hour after hour we pushed. Now and then we slid past or had to veer around barely submerged rocks. Instead of innocent, smooth, round boulders, they looked split, up-ended and jagged, lying in ambush to tear a slit in our canvas-bottomed canoes. In bright sunlight an alert bowman could steer us around them safely, but as the twilight deepened we had to proceed with more and more caution. Finally it became so dark that we were probing and feeling on every stroke.

By eleven o'clock we had almost made the crossing, but we could go no farther. On a lake with low brushy shore lines finding a campsite in daylight is difficult. Now there were no distinguishing landmarks. We could tell what was land and what was water, but that was about all. Skirting the shore line, we directed the beams of flashlights into the blackness until we finally picked out what seemed to be a sand beach. A landing showed it to be only a narrow strip with dense brush coming almost to the water's edge. No place for tents. After another half-hour of searching and probing into bays we gave up, returned to our sand beach, unloaded and began hacking out some semblance of clearing in the undergrowth. By midnight the entire crew was dragging and irritable. With three of the four tents pitched we doubled up for an uncomfortable night, with twigs and stubs of saplings poking into ribs and backs.

In the morning there was sand in the food, sand in the dunnage, sand in everything. And Fred, our key bowman, came reeling out of the tent ashen and with no interest in breakfast. He had been sick all night. Too many eggs!

A stiff but uneventful paddle put us safely across the rest of Touchwood to the entrance of the short, fast-flowing continuation of the Mink River. A few riffles and then came the one portage around the rapids called Wesachewan: "Swift current running into a bay." And then we blew into God's Lake across the bay, on the heels of a sudden thunderstorm, and landed on its smooth sand beach, a rarity in rock country.

God's Lake is 50 miles long and 35 across at its widest point. It's a big lake to cross, but it was more than that to us. It meant the completion of the first lap of our journey. This first 250 miles had been primarily lake-to-lake travel with portages and relatively small streams as connecting links. From here on we would be leaving the lake route. The roaring God's River would give us a fast ride down to York Factory on Hudson Bay. From the Bay, by a laborious upstream journey, the Nelson River would lead us back to Norway House.

Our first two weeks on the trail signified the first lap for another reason; this hop of 250 miles was the distance between settlements. No one lives on the route over which we had come from Norway House; the God's Lake settlement—a Hudson's Bay Company outpost—was an oasis in the wilderness.

The very idea of a trading post fired the boys with so much enthusiasm that they paddled the last fourteen miles scarcely missing a stroke. If there was a store, there would be something to buy.

The moccasin telegraph, a mysteriously fast word-of-mouth communication system, had been in operation. The settlement knew that we were coming, and the Indians camped around the post could tell by the style in which we swung our paddles that white men were approaching. The sled-dogs howled to announce our arrival. Indian families piled out of tents to line the banks, and the post manager was on the dock to greet us.

Our crew had had visions of an honest-to-goodness store with well-stocked shelves filled with food unavailable on the trail, but they were in for a let-down. In the wilderness outposts, supplies are freighted in by canoe for hundreds of miles or flown in occasionally in limited amounts, so they are meager at the best. But just now the situation was at its worst. Treaty money had recently been paid. Once a year the Canadian government pays every treaty Indian the amount due him, and also doles out to needy families supplies such as flour and new fish nets. It is a gala occasion for which members of the tribe may travel hundreds of miles to celebrate for a week at their annual get-together. Needless to say they had spent their treaty money. The Company shelves were almost bare.

That would not stop our boys. Snarkey started the idea, and to the last man the others followed him. No candy or ice cream? Well, then they would stock up on honey and jam, cheese and cookies.

"But all of that is in our grub," said Ben. "You get it as part of your meals."

"Well, but Chief," Chuck explained, "if we *own* a five-pound jar of jam, we can eat it all at one sitting if we want to, without having to share it with eleven other people."

Ben scouted around until he found Pete Burton, a veteran woodsman and trapper, who was a good man for questioning about the North country.

"Well, as long as you're goin' the direction I'm headed," Pete said thoughtfully, "I just might come along with you a ways. Don't often find myself company into the woods. Might kinda like it for a change."

The boys had hurried off to the postmaster's office to see what the mail situation was like. They returned with half-amused, half-puzzled looks. "He says there hasn't been a mail delivery since last March! But we can write home if we want to. Any odd plane that happens to land will pick up the outgoing mail."

"How do people live without mail?" Frederic wondered.

"Now, I'll tell you why the government don't send it," said Pete. "There's only five white people living on God's Lake. 'Tain't profitable, that's what. Indians don't write each other much," he added, chuckling.

We spoke briefly with the Mounted Police officer stationed at the settlement. Chuck was anxious to know what he did with his time. There wasn't much to waste, the Mounty told us. There might not be many people in his territory—fifty-seven whites and a few hundred Indians—but thirty thousand square miles was a lot of territory to keep under law and order. To say nothing of taking the census! We were all impressed. One man to handle a district the size of the state of Indiana!

The campsite for which we headed was one that Ben had used many times. Ferrier's Island, the natives call it. Chuck and Franklin had been there with him the previous year. "Think you can find it?" he asked them.

The other boys chortled. "Now we'll see how good you really are!"

There were hundreds of islands of all shapes and sizes. The sky was overcast; another storm was brewing. The light was poor. But after heading for a few spots that resembled our island, the navigators suddenly let out a triumphant "Yahoo!" and took us straight to it.

For the next two days a terrific storm whipped and swept across God's Lake. We had planned on a day's lay-over here because our crew was sorely in need of another intensive session of coaching in canoemanship before starting down God's River. Days off are few and far between; I had counted on catching up on the family washing. But there was no coaching and no washing. For two days we huddled around camp in the rain. The northeaster lashed the whole lake into a fury of ten-foot waves. The canoes were carried back into the bush and tied to trees for good measure.

Against the force of the gale out on the points we had to brace ourselves to keep from being blown off the rocks. Voices disappeared in thin air. We had to shout to be heard.

Whenever you have the hard luck to be windbound and confined to camp in a rain storm, it is unwise to try to seek shelter inside a tent. There is not enough light to read or play cards. Sitting on the ground you soon become chilled and stiff. There is an unwritten camp rule that no one step inside a tent with wet muddy feet. Rather than tracking in and out, it is preferable to dress appropriately to brave the elements, and, once you are out in the morning, to stay out and keep as active as possible.

There was plenty of exercise in keeping up an adequate wood supply for an all-day warming and drying fire. Our fishing enthusiasts spent hours casting off shore and brought in enough nice walleyed pike to provide a good fish-fry. The botanists set up their improvised shelter, lit their stove and worked steadily to dry their precious specimens.

The Hudson's Bay Company post manager had told us of gold on Ferrier's Island. Prospectors had already staked claims. In the granite shield which fans out from Canada's southern boundary to cover vast expanses of the northern wilderness, the basic rock, the original earth's crust with all its ores and elements, is exposed to the surface for all comers to see—though it was not until air transportation came along that the country became accessible and a start made on development of its great resources.

An Indian, if asked how God's Lake and God's River got the name, will tell you that it means "Land of Plenty." Plenty fur, plenty game. Big otter, big fish. To this the white man adds, plenty gold. And bush prospectors and trappers, with their infinite patience and powers of observation, have made some rich and important finds.

"How much are we sleeping on, Chief?" the boys wondered.

"A quarter of a million dollars, I hear," grinned Ben.

By afternoon of the second stormbound day every inch of Ferrier's Island had been explored. Nobody, unfortunately, picked up any nuggets.

That evening the boys did not attack their meals with their usual gusto; nor did they seem very happy. Four of them had acquired a tell-tale sickly green cast and pale lips. Their private stock of jam, cheese and cookies was taking its toll.

"I think I've got the gut-rot," said Snarkey weakly.

"Don't be inelegant," said Steve. "But I guess I have, too. Gut-rot it is."

"But it's worth it," said Chuck. "That jam was swell!"

With the wind still howling we huddled around the fire and listened to Ben tell tales of the Crees and their beliefs. To understand the Indian, he said, the white man must take into account the important role that the Witigo plays in Indian life.

"The Witigo?"

"Well—listen!" said Ben.

"The forms that the creature may take are legion. It may be a grotesque white man. Some say it is cannibalistic and eats human flesh. Others describe it as a ghost that turns up at any time of day or night to haunt and follow you. If the Indian doesn't actually see the Witigo, he is given the dire warnings by finding signs of his presence. On one of those days when everything seems to go wrong, it is the Witigo, lurking unseen, that bedevils and plagues him.

"There is the story of David Curlyhead. David took his canoe and started off over God's Lake to go hunting. On the way he landed at a small bare rock island where gulls were nesting. A gust of wind blew his canoe away. It was forty days before he was found, a sick and exhausted man. His only food had been gulls' eggs. The Witigo had snatched his canoe and almost got him but he lived because he was in the Land of Plenty.

"Because of the Witigo there was a period of several years when the Indians would not go near God's River. It seems that a white trapper had a pair of worn-out rubber boots. Having no use for them, he left them, bottom side up, on two sticks near the entrance to the river. Indians coming along saw two boots with water lapping around them and fled from what they supposed to be a dead man with feet pointing skyward. It was the work of the Witigo. As long as the boots were there, no Indian dared venture near God's River."

The crossing of God's Lake is a challenge even in fair weather. In the past two weeks we had had the experience of navigating over big bodies of water, but this was the granddaddy of them all. Its hundreds of islands, large and small, with their rocky points worn smooth by the action of water and ice, are covered with a dense growth of small trees. Its waters are clear and cold. And it is deep—three hundred feet in some places. We were to see only a small portion of it even though we pushed off at six in the morning with a fair day's paddle to God's River.

We had twelve more miles of the lake to cross, six of them strung with a chain of islands that could offer protection against unruly elements, and then six miles of open water; nothing but water on the horizon. "You'll not see that again till you see the ocean," said the Chief.

"The ocean!" It was easy to forget in this constant river travel that the turning point of our journey was Hudson Bay. We would see plenty of ocean, and canoe in it when we swung from York Factory around the Bay to the Nelson River.

Before we left the last little island for the long open stretch, Ben called, "Time out for fishing!" A chorus of cheers answered him.

God's Lake, even in its remoteness, cannot be classified as virgin waters. Since the nineteen-thirties it has been commercially fished. It is claimed that nets have yielded lake trout and northern pike weighing up to fifty and sixty pounds. Though these records have never been equaled on rod and reel, our crew had been yearning to try their luck.

Almost as fast as bait was cast out—zing! A bent rod, a tussle to reel in the line. The water was so clear that we could watch the beauties as they were brought closer and closer. They were all running about the same size, eight to nine pounds.

As a safety measure Ben does not permit the use of landing nets or gaff hooks. With the temptation to lean out over the side with net or hook, there is too much danger of tipping. The same technique was used on these fighting prizes as on all other fish. They were reeled in alongside and brought in with a skillful scoop of the hand without a shift of balance. There was no need to fish deep even in the middle of July. In these icy waters the trout were right on the surface.

"We take no more than we can use," Ben told the fishermen. "No real sportsmen ever do. If any of you have brought along an attitude that anything that swims is to be caught or anything that flies or has fur is to be shot, you'll have to get over it, or be mighty unhappy with us. Fish for fun, sure, as well as for food. But when we have enough to eat, the rest of the catch is to go back into the lake."

Our crew was rapidly learning how to fish for fun with the least injury to the fish. File the barbs off the hooks so that the mouth parts will not be torn in removing them. Wet your hands so they will not stick to the skin and rub off the protective coat of slime. Denuded of this slimy coat, fish become a likely target for parasites and bacteria from which they later sicken and die. Remember that if you throw the fish back into the water with a powerful heave, you may rupture the air sacs. Handle them carefully, and if they show signs of sluggishness, place them back in the water and gently stroke the belly toward the gills to revive them.

Directly ahead of us now was the rampaging God's River. Ben ordered an intensive coaching session at the first rapids. These were tricky, but safe; made to order for learning. Swinging around a bend they boiled and rolled downhill, but there was a well-defined chute to follow and enough water so that there was no danger of hitting rocks. What made this an ideal practice grounds was that the run was a short one, and along the shore there was an eddy. At the end of the fast downstream ride it was possible to swing into the eddy, paddle upstream with comparative ease, and then, by putting on steam, once again break into the chute. At the top, where the canoe nosed out of the eddy with a sharp right turn, there were strong crosscurrents. A canoe tips into the current as it swings, and it was necessary here to shift balance by leaning to the left just enough to counteract the tip and bring things back on an even keel.

Taking the lead canoe we ran it through a few times

as a demonstration. The two middlemen took no part whatsoever. We just sat in the bottom, hung on, and watched the shore fly by, while the bow- and stern-men did all the work.

Trip after trip we all made, *Esox, Shekel* and *Chief*. Around and around, while Ben kept at us. "Veteran river men have great respect for white water. Don't get to thinking you have nothing to worry about. The God's River can subdue anybody if it takes a notion."

Down the river just at that moment came Pete Burton to join us. "Evenin', everybody! What's matter, Ben? You look mighty serious."

"I am, Pete. And you're just the person to help drive my point home. Veteran woodsmen have respect for white water, eh, Pete?"

Pete said quietly, "I wear a life-vest myself."

There were raised eyebrows and thoughtful looks at that. And no mutterings about getting on with the trip. The boys practically lined up for practice.

"Remember," Ben told them, "if you have no conception of the dangers in this business, you might be careless. Now you have no reason to be. If you take nothing seriously, you're apt to wind up in the drink. But I think even the craziest of you takes survival seriously." He whacked Snarkey across the shoulders. "And finally, I hope none of you is likely to lose his head in an emergency. From what I've seen so far, you're as steady a crew as I've ever known. Who wants to be first?"

Veterans Don't Have Adventures

THERE WAS ANOTHER SESSION OF PRACTICE THE NEXT morning before breakfast. "We can't leave camp until everyone demonstrates what he can do," declared Ben. He started with Walt and Chuck—Walt in the stern, Chuck in the bow position. They made a successful run and then paddled upstream in the eddy to make a repeat trip. As they nosed out of the eddy into the crosscurrents, Walt leaned in the wrong direction.

Above the sound of the rushing water we heard a yell. Tip-over! At almost the same instant Ben and John grabbed a beached canoe and shoved off into the swirling river after them.

The rest of us froze. Chuck and Walt, hanging on to the overturned canoe for dear life, were bouncing crazily through those icy waters at the mercy of the current. The waves rolled around and over them. The distance between them and our camp lengthened. Now we saw the bobbing heads, now we didn't. Up—down—there they are! Where are they?

When Ben and John reached them, they were being carried swiftly to another rapids down below. The current was too wild to do more than grab the painter, tie it and take the men in tow to keep them from being swept on downstream. With an arm locked around a thwart and clutching to the gunwale, each of them still had his paddle in a firm grasp.

With all that extra weight behind, Ben and John had a tough time making headway. They were carried almost a mile below camp before they could reach land.

Breakfast was a sober affair. What had started as a practice rapids turned out to be just that in a way not planned on—it had demonstrated how tragedies occur. It illustrated a favorite point of Ben's, that there is no time to stop and figure out the next move. The skills of canoemanship have to be there and made use of in split-second decisions. The God's River was not the place to learn by making mistakes.

After breakfast there was a solemn meeting. How had tragedy been averted? By following to the letter the age-old safety rule: in case of a tip-over, hang on to the paddle and grab the canoe; never leave it and attempt to swim to shore. Why had the accident occurred? Lack of that all-important sense of balance? Carelessness? What was it?

"As I've said before," Ben spoke almost too quietly, "an adventure is a mark of incompetence. Stefansson said it first; I can't say it enough. I have no intention of risking life and limb to reach our goal. Every man must know his role and show that he is capable of putting to use the skills and techniques he has learned before we're ready to take on what lies ahead. We'll have another hour's practice starting now!"

It was overcast and chilly, the weather matching our mood, as we finally started off on the second lap. A good three hundred and fifty canoe miles stretched between us and York Factory on Hudson Bay. The God's River was seldom traveled by either Indian or white. The long stretch was uninhabited except for a small trading post and settlement at Shamattawa, two hundred miles away.

From here to the Bay the river drops 585 feet. There are no falls of any account. It just rolls downhill. In a country where it rains on an average of one day out of three, and where the lakes and rivers cover nearly half the earth's surface, terrific volume is inevitable. White water, white water, white water. Mile after mile after mile. To be comparable, the great Mississippi, instead of dropping 782 feet in its 2,000-mile course from Minneapolis to the Gulf of Mexico, would have to drop 3,200 feet. The Father of Waters meanders and spreads over the countryside on its way to the Gulf. The God's River surges between banks often no more than 200 yards apart.

From the time we had left camp the rapids came

thick and fast for several hours. Instead of three canoes there were now four in the flotilla. Pete's little
craft seemed dwarfed by our freighters. Paddling all
by himself, he had no difficulty in keeping pace with
us. Sure enough, he wore a life-vest.

With the middlemen walking along shore to
lighten the weight by a few hundred pounds, the first
rapids was run with loaded canoes. At the second rapids the waves and backwash were rolling so high that
there was danger of the bow plowing under instead of
riding buoyantly over the top. We unloaded and portaged all the gear. Ben and Franklin ran the three
emptied canoes through a beautiful chute past a rock
pile.

As we approached the third rapids, which was
much too wild to run, the current was terrific. To
keep from being swept out into it, we resorted to the
technique known as bushwhacking for several hundred feet before landing to make the portage. Instead
of paddling we hugged the shore, hanging to branches
of willow shrubs and alder bushes. Bushwhacking at
the speed we were going was tricky business. The
stern had to be pointed in toward shore and the bow
slightly out. If our tail end had nosed out into that
current, in a flash we would have found ourselves going downstream backwards. Grabbing frantically at
the branches as we flew past resulted in scratched and
cut hands for members of the crew who had not had
the foresight to put on gloves. The first aid kit came
out when we stopped for lunch.

Conversations and discussions around the fire at meal time cover a multitude of subjects. This time it turned to fish and fishing. The Chief was being grilled. Where were those big ones he talked about sometimes? Hadn't he said he'd seen brook trout twenty-six inches long, weighing eight pounds?

Ben laughed. "Oh, I'll have to straighten you out! Those eight-pounders were not only rare. They were phenomenal.

"The whole thing in a nutshell amounts to this. Generally speaking, the farther north you go, the poorer the fishing becomes. Many a sportsman has the erroneous notion that if he could only find a secluded spot that no one else knew about and where he could have a whole lake or stream to himself, it would be paradise. He could, if he chose, haul them in by the boatload. But you don't see any fishermen around here, do you? Not in all the miles we've come. That's partly because these waters are not teeming with fish. There isn't sufficient food to support a large fish population."

The reason? Topography. The bottoms as well as the shores of most of the lakes in this part of Canada, Ben said, are clean granite rock. The necessary mud, vegetation, crawfish, small minnows and insect larva, the ideal spawning beds of sand and gravel, just are not there.

The combination of cold water and scarce amounts of food means slow growth. So the waters of the Canadian shield, or rock area, even in southern Canada and northern Minnesota, cannot stand pounding by large numbers of sportsmen. If a road is built into previously untouched lakes of the region or planes allowed to land, after a few years the lake is fished out.

As we pushed on, the afternoon brought a respite from the tension of navigating the white water of the rapids. The river widened and smoothed out. The current carried us along at a good clip without much effort on our part. It was a relief to be able to relax and take notice of the world about us; the physical characteristics, the fauna and flora. After God's Lake the topography changed rapidly. Over the shield of solid granite was an overburden of clay, sand and gravel. Rocky shores were being replaced by low clay banks. The river bottom changed to sand and gravel with occasional outcroppings of rock to keep us on our toes. For the first time since leaving Norway House we saw no hills of granite in the background. Little streams trickling in on both sides of God's River were numerous, clear and ice-cold, for their source was the melting ice of muskeg.

This clay sand and gravel country offered better spawning grounds for the fish. There was good reason why those speckled trout found it a spot to their liking. As we paddled along, the backs of whitefish and red-finned mullets broke the water briefly. Now and then we glimpsed the dark bodies of some big fellows appearing to be eight- or ten-pounders. They were black suckers.

This was an important transition zone for our plant

collectors. For them it meant a spell of feverish activity making detailed notes of the changes in conditions for plant growth and keeping their eyes peeled for new specimens. Traveling through country untouched as far as previous botanical research was concerned they were most anxious to carry back as complete and accurate a picture as possible.

According to their maps, which were supposedly authentic, we were already beyond the conifers. In fact, those maps showed us to be in treeless tundra. Nothing could be further from the truth, although the timber was becoming noticeably smaller as we pushed northward. We still had three hundred and fifty miles to go and we would have trees all the way regardless of what the map showed.

Here the forest growth was dense. Of the conifers, spruce was, as usual, dominant. But there were sprinklings of jack pine, balsam, tamarack and creeping juniper. Alder, birch, willows and poplar lined the shores. A find of the day—a species not noted before —was one lone mountain ash about ten feet high. How did it get there? Mere speculation was that birds feeding on the bright-colored berries may fly considerable distances carrying and dropping the seeds.

Two bald eagles, handsome, powerful fellows, easily identified by their white heads and tails, circled, swooped, and then soared so high that they became mere specks. We did not see them again, but all day we were convoyed by circling, swooping, diving terns.

This was the season when many of the ducks are in

eclipse plumage. They were not so colorful as they appear to be in bird-book pictures. The gaudy feathers of the drakes had been replaced by much duller hues. With flight feathers shed they could not fly until they had grown new ones. The birds in this predicament flopped and scooted rather helplessly but always managed to keep a safe distance from us.

During the afternoon we began to sight for the first time the white-winged scoter. Rather than traveling singly or in pairs they always seem to congregate by the dozens. We did not see the young, however, and so we thought these flocks were roving bachelor males; the nesting ground must be elsewhere. When the scoters take off in flight they tilt as simultaneously as a well-trained chorus line, until they seem to be standing on the very tips of their toes to shake the water from their wings. When disturbed by our approach, instead of circling and gaining altitude, they fly so close to the water that their wingtips touch the waves as they beat a retreat; then they settle in again at a safe distance.

"You know," said John thoughtfully, "for some reason, the sky seems lower here than it is at home. Leaving science out of the picture, I wonder if it could be that the farther north we travel the nearer we come to the top of the world?"

Nobody laughed at him. It was something that had been sensed by all of us. Here in the wilderness preserved intact as created, unaltered by man, we are closer to the heavens—and to the earth. Surrounded on all sides by creation, we become aware of our relation to the universe and of our life's span to infinity. We learn that we are really dependent on nature, even when we live in the city. We understand the source of everything that belongs to mankind. We know that it isn't man-made.

"Yes," someone agreed, and the rest of us nodded. "Science or not, I think the sky is mighty close to us here, too."

When our craft had reached relatively safe waters again, Pete drew alongside in his little canoe for a chat. A source of unlimited authentic information, he was being bombarded with questions. From him we learned that all good trappers lately had been doing "right well." The previous season a good beaver skin had brought as much as ninety-two dollars and a mink from fifty to seventy-five dollars. In addition to these, the traps yield otter, weasel, red fox, cross fox, fisher and occasionally a marten. Wolverines, that plague of trappers? Well, they were rare in these parts.

For meat the native depends largely on moose, for this is not deer or caribou country. In all of his years in the God's Lake area Pete had seen less than a dozen woodland caribou. The previous winter, for the first time, he had witnessed a migration of sizable herds of the Barren Land caribou. By the thousands they had come down from the Barren Lands, their route following, in general, the tractor train "roads" into God's River country. Behind them they had left the snow trampled down to the hardness of pavement, and in their wake came packs of wolves.

On the practical side, Pete gave the boys a lesson in setting rabbit snares. In the deep moss of the North country the trampled trails of the snow-shoe rabbit are well defined and easy to spot. A loop of thin pliable copper wire is suspended from branches over the runway. The unsuspecting bunny hopping along the trail sticks his head into the loop. In his struggle to get free, the noose tightens. This simple piece of equipment, weighing practically nothing and carried in a pocket at all times, can be a means of survival in the wilderness for a man stranded without sufficient food. In case of necessity a stripped spruce root or even a thong lacing of a moccasin can be substituted for wire. To Pete this was not a theory. He had used it more than once.

The God's River was ready to dish out some of the real McCoy as we started off on the second day. There was seriousness and tension in the crew, and the weather lent an atmosphere of gloom. Though the thermometer told us it was 50°, a chilly mist that enveloped us made us feel as though we were wrapped in clammy wet sheets. Frank managed to get a laugh out of twelve rather grumpy people when he discovered a white-footed mouse in his dunnage. The mouse had had a busy night shredding toilet tissue to fashion a nice cozy nest. It isn't every day that a mouse can get even with a mouse collector.

Beyond our sand beach camp, the river narrowed once again, its waters confined between clay banks. The more it narrowed, the faster it flew. Bang, bang, bang on the heels of one rapids came another one. On a twisting course there were no long vistas to give much warning of what we were getting into. This meant crossing and recrossing the river, swinging wide to peer around the corners.

Through the years the natives have given names to some of the doozers. The first one of any account that we came to they call Gentleman's Rapids. If ever there was a misnomer, that is it. There is nothing honorable about it. No gentleman would sneak up on you unaware and slap you. If we had not been well to the outside of that particularly sharp bend we would have been in a fix. Beyond the chute, which we had hit right on the nose, the waves were four to five feet high, the shore flew by, and we cleared water and hit it again with teeth-jarring bounces.

About two hours out of camp there was a sharp bend to the left. We veered to make tracks for the right-hand shore to have a look at what was in store for us. At the rate at which we were being hurtled downstream we had started the crossing too late. Just about midstream Allen's Rapids came to meet us. Rocks, rocks, everywhere, with shallow white water swirling around them. There was no channel. Our heavily-loaded freighters couldn't make it. Those rocks would slash the canvas-bottomed canoes to ribbons.

"Jump!" shouted the Chief.

Over the sides we went—in the nick of time.

This was no place for the weaker sex. I was told to get myself on land and stay there. By grabbing at rocks when the current threatened to sweep me off my feet, I managed to wade in to shore.

Meanwhile the men out in midstream were probing for holes between the boulders wide enough and deep enough to float the lightened canoes. Keeping the bows parallel to the current, alternately pulling and pushing and crabbing sidewise, they finally reached the deep channel where the waters of God's River were playing crack-the-whip on the curve along the right-hand shore. They were out of one tight spot only to find themselves in another. Now stepping into holes well over their heads, they clutched at the gunwales to keep from being swept downstream. Too rocky to run. Too deep to wade. Utterly impossible to portage through an impenetrable thicket of brush, high as a tall man's head, that came to the water's edge. There was one solution—the technique of roping.

This was tricky business. With no one riding, the canoes were lowered through the fast water by directing and controlling the course with ropes—one tied to the front thwart and passing out through the bow plate ring, the other fastened to the back thwart. In roping, the load must be distributed so that the bow rides higher than the stern. If the stern swung out and the canoe turned broadside, the strength of four men would not be enough to keep it from being swept out into the raging river. With two men manning the ropes from shore where they could get firm footing, two additional men waded, grasping the gunwales and weaving in and out to avoid crashing on the rocks. The ropes, held taut, were brought in or let out as necessary. By this combination of brakes and rudders the battle to conquer Upper Allen's Rapids went on and on.

When at last we had made it, our ordeal was still only half over. A few hundred yards ahead was Lower Allen's Rapids—more treacherous than the white water just conquered. There was no way of getting through on this right side. The river was about one-eighth of a mile wide. In the swirling current, we had to make the crossing. Pointing the bows upstream at a 45° angle, we paddled furiously to keep from being carried into the rampaging white waters below. We nosed straight into the clay bank; the bowmen jumped and hung on for dear life while the rest of us scrambled on all fours over the heaps of dunnage to join them.

Here on the left-hand shore, the canoes had to be lowered once again by roping. With the current even more powerful than it had been in the upper rapids, the job took six men instead of four. The brush came to the water's edge and the men on the ropes were continually getting tangled in the branches. If the other four had been monkeys it would have helped, for their job was to hold the canoe off shore, leaping over shrubbery, working from fantastic positions, and using paddles as bumpers.

And hoofing along slippery twenty-foot banks and wading the waist-deep icy streams that poured into God's River was no fun for us extra hands. We all had a cross to bear.

The morning had been an endurance contest. Fortunately, Allen's Rapids was the last one of the day. The high banks flattened to become low, grassy, willow-fringed shores. Except for an occasional outcropping, the parent rock was covered by an overburden of sand and gravel. Several times the river widened to such an extent that it took on the appearance of a lake. In placid waters and with the current to help push, we were really traveling. After the trials of the morning it was a treat to watch the shore slip by with so little effort. The boys swung their paddles rhythmically, keeping time as they sang about cruising down the river on a Sunday afternoon.

Here on the God's River there was an abundance of waterfowl, and at this season, when the ducklings were small and their mothers hung close, it was no trick to list the area as a nesting grounds for half-a-dozen or more species. Of others, there were only adults; and of still others which we had seen in past years, none at all. Waterfowl population is governed by weather conditions, water levels and food supplies, and an area which is well-populated one season may

Ben and Marion Ferrier.

The Ferrier Crew. (Left to right) John Olmsted, Orwin Rustad, Arthur Eschbach, Walter Eschbach, Charles Albright, Marion Ferrier, Adlai E. Stevenson III, William K. Kellogg III, Franklin Dunbaugh, Charles Nadler, Fred Hord.

A loaded canoe early in the trip.

Beaching a canoe at Painted Stone.

Portage: the tumpline in operation.

Portage: canoe carry at Logon Lake.

Campsite.

Ben in his tent.

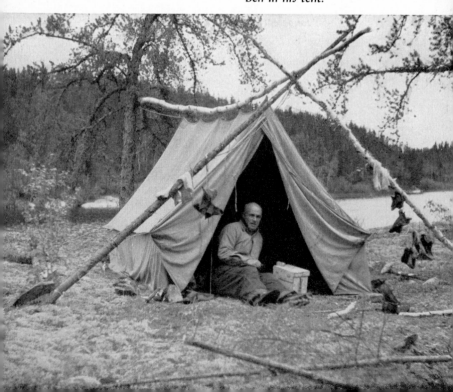

Canoe ready for portage.

Dingle—three pots.

Reflector Dingle.

A fisherman's reward: speckled trout steaks.

Entering rapids.

In the midst of rapids.

Stranded on the floor of Hudson Bay in a fog
and with a storm approaching.

Tracking along the Nelson River.

Lining a heavy freighter upstream on the Nelson River.

The last lap of the trip: boarding the Muskeg Special at Mile 352 of the Churchill Railroad.

be completely by-passed the next. You won't find ten thousand ducks in an area that will support only a few hundred. Northern Manitoba, in spite of being a maze of waterways, provides neither abundant nesting grounds nor food. It is too clean.

Ducks, migrating along the central flyways, veer off to the north and west of Lake Winnipeg to concentrate by the millions in the sloughs, pot-holes and marshes of the prairie provinces of Alberta and Saskatchewan where they find mud bottoms, shallow shores, luxuriant ground cover and food: duckweed, sago pondweed, smartweed. The geese choose their homes near the shores of Hudson Bay or keep right on going until they reach the islands north of the continent.

On the third day's run the river was increasing in volume and speed. We traveled at such a smart clip that we were barely limbered up before we saw the snorting white waters of Boiling Rapids. Across its entire width the God's River tumbled over irregularly spaced rocks. A whole series of miniature falls formed a graceful semicircle. Some distance below the falls the white waters converged with a tremendous swirl and backwash, the spray flying in all directions. Landing for the portage, we took time to stand and gaze.

"I saw a man run this once in a fifteen-foot ratting canoe," Ben remarked. "Karl Bayly—he was one of the best white-water men ever to hit the North. I considered myself quite an expert till I traveled with Karl for two weeks. That set me back on my heels! He had techniques I'd never heard of. I guess, though, the most valuable thing I learned from him was that a good canoeman knows his capabilities and never takes a chance. One mistake in judgment is all that's necessary to leave a pile of ribs—canoe ribs and human ribs mixed up and washed ashore as tangible evidence to a searching party that you weren't as good as you thought you were. Shows you how good Karl was; he knew he could run this." Ben paused, then smiled. "I have no intention of running Boiling Rapids!"

7

Rapids Can Be Run

THE CONDITION OF THE PORTAGE WAS CONVINCING proof that we would not be bothered by any traffic on the God's River. No one passing in either direction could get around this spot except by tramping over the portage as we were doing. There was not the slightest trace of a path—no footprints, trampled grass or broken twigs to give any indication of how long it had been since human feet had trod this way. The Chief and Pete headed off through the thick growth of brush to reconnoiter. They returned with the news that those of us carrying packs might possibly be able to bulldoze through, but they would have to take time out to hack out a swath for the men carrying the canoes.

The tough portage put us safely beyond the falls of Boiling Rapids. But the old river kept right on boiling. Not only did those wild, foaming rapids stretch as far as eye could see, but as we were to find out, they went on for miles and miles. With gear stacked and ready to reload, the Chief held a conclave to give out instructions.

"Once launched there will be no turning back; no time to change your mind and decide to do it some other way, no possibility of portaging or landing to figure out what to do next. In the next few miles everything you've been taught about white-water canoeing will be put to a test.

"These rapids can be run. Whether they are safe or suicidal depends on judgment, skill and trigger-fast reactions. A spot like this calls for a perfectly balanced load side to side and front to back, with the bow riding slightly higher than the stern. All the middlemen are excess baggage. Just crouch in the bottom so you won't obstruct the view; you'll help keep the ballast low! Don't wiggle or gawp around to find out how your pals in the rear are making out. One squirm at the wrong moment could mean disaster. I think you know that."

Maneuvering at such speed would require perfect team work by bow and stern paddlers. Ben, in the stern of the lead canoe, would concentrate on the general course, watching the behavior of the water in the distance, picking the chutes and spotting danger signs before it was too late to do something about them. How we came through depended on his ability to read water like the pages of a book. A resurgent heave, a spout, a savage curling and licking, a bulge, a sudden swerve of the current, a glassy smoothness, a change in appearance of the shore line on the horizon —all had meaning and had to be interpreted in terms of safety.

The other canoes were to follow his course as exactly as possible. To avoid a pile-up in case of trouble, there was to be an interval of at least fifty yards between each canoe. All bowmen were warned once again that, in fast water, they have the tremendous responsibility of being the rock-dodgers. The bowman's view of whatever looms up directly ahead is unobstructed. Not only is he in a position to see a menacing boulder sooner, but at such speed, it would be utterly impossible for the stern helmsman to change direction of a heavily-loaded canoe fast enough to dodge it. The kind of steering it takes to swerve sharply to the right or left in white water is done by the man in the front seat. If at any time a crash seems inevitable, he has to take it head on, jump just before the nose hits, brace himself on the rock and keep the bow pointing straight into the current while he lifts it off.

"That water is really in a hurry to get where it's going, isn't it?" Steve was pretty solemn.

"It is," Ben agreed. "And it means you've got to shoot straight. Unless you want to find yourselves being tossed around and turning sidewise, remember, your speed has to exceed that of the current. Going downstream broadside at such a rate, through a rock-strewn rapids, is a sure way of wrecking a canoe, losing all supplies and jeopardizing lives. You want to eat tonight?"

Fred, as key bowman in the lead canoe, was apprehensive and none too happy. "You'll be fine," Ben assured him. "I shuffle our crews around now and then, as you've seen, till I have an idea of how they might work the best. I wouldn't have you here if I didn't think you could do it."

To say that during the next hour we had a fast ride is a gross understatement. We crossed and recrossed that river, swinging from one channel and chute to another, dodging rocks all the way. I couldn't see the rocks, but I could watch Fred's paddle fly. A sudden reversal of the position of his hands—a reaching forward and out to the side with the tip of the blade pointing ahead of the bow—a powerful pull, and we shot left. A swing of the paddle—the same cross-bow rudder stroke on the opposite side, and we swerved right. Meanwhile, each time the bow zigged or zagged to miss a juicy boulder, Ben, in the stern, was left to provide the power for forward motion to keep us moving faster than the current. At the same time he had to follow through with a fish-tail stroke to bring us back on course or we would have been hurtled sidewise.

To make himself heard over the roar of the rapids he was shouting directions at the top of his lungs. "Paddle, Fred! Paddle harder! Faster! Draw right." With both of them reaching far out to the same side, a powerful sweep of the flat surface of the blade brought the whole length of the canoe into a sideslip crabwise as they aimed for the next chute.

At times I just crouched and hung on. When it wasn't too wild I could not resist the temptation to crane my neck and peek to see what was coming next. Where would I go if I were in the driver's seat? Had I been the navigator we could have been shipwrecked and drowned a dozen times. The whole thing had me completely baffled. One side of the river would be as smooth as syrup and the other side rolling to beat thunder as far as you could see and on around a bend. It seemed utterly insane to go out into that torrent when it was so calm and peaceful on the other side. But out we went. I didn't need to ask why. At the end of the nice smooth syrup there was a three-foot falls that I hadn't even seen. What a mess that would have been—one smashed canoe and two more piling on top of us. Now I knew all about it. All you have to do is avoid smooth water and aim for the waves and whitecaps.

By that time we had come to the bend. That was simple. In downstream travel you swing wide, not only to be able to see what is ahead, but because it is more navigable on that side. The water, sweeping around the curve, plays crack-the-whip and gouges out a deeper channel. Surely that was where they would go. But no. In a flash they were heading furiously for the middle. Good reason. We just missed a jagged rock ledge jutting out, with the old river tumbling off its edge in a drop that would have meant disaster. Once again I was wrong. You don't always stick to the outside of a bend.

Ahead now was a straightaway. I could see white foam spewing up all over the place, with blue water and a racing current on both sides. If waves meant deep water and a safe chute, that was the spot. But Ben and Fred swerved far to the left to avoid it.

I couldn't stand it any longer. I yelled back to Ben. "Why didn't you take that nice chute?"

By his tone of voice I gathered that he was thoroughly disgusted with my stupidity. "That was no chute! Furthermore those were spouts, not waves! There were rocks just a few inches below the surface. When water hits rocks going that fast it has to go someplace. So it goes straight up!"

I should have let it drop right there, but I persisted. "Where it hit the rocks and bounced up in the air— was that what you call a backwash?"

I should have put cotton in my ears against the language used to answer that one. The gist of it was that a backwash comes at the end of a drop and the water curls over and back upstream. I could see that this wasn't the time to press for any more valuable information on canoemanship.

When it was all over we nosed into shore for a landing to rest and relax. Fred was pale and a little shaky. The adventure had taxed both physical strength and nerves. The Chief gave him a healthy whack on the back. "Thanks, Fred. I'd have been helpless without a key bowman who was on his toes every second."

The men of the *Esox* and *Shekel* came in for their share of praise for the masterful job they had done in playing follow the leader. They too had come through without a scratch.

Pete had wisely chosen to bring up the rear. "Didn't care to be in the path of them loaded freighters," he explained. "You guys are pretty good for city folks, though."

One supper time while Pete was with us, twelve people started firing questions at him about the life of a trapper. He was hard to jog into steady conversation, but once he was started, he could make a speech as fervent as any of Ben's. "And I'll tell you young fellas something you better not forget, especially since you've got more of an interest in the future now than us old-timers have."

"What's that, Pete?"

"Laws are made to insure a continuous supply of wildlife. If sportsmen don't stop slaughterin' they won't have nothin' to kill after awhile. Though I ain't one for sayin' those kind of folks deserve the name of sportsmen, anyhow.

"Now you take the Canadian trappin' regulations. They're good, and they're enforced. Stiff enforcement. Every man licensed to trap has a well-defined territory and it belongs to him and nobody else. His catch is limited according to species. He's got to maintain his line according to the rules. And the Indians have got to be protected, too. Government's not giving any more licenses to white men now. I'm one of few white trappers left around this territory."

Franklin stuffed his mouth full just as he thought of a question, and had a hard time swallowing everything fast enough.

"Take it easy, Piggy!"

"Quiet, son. Pete, how do you work when you run your line? How can you count on the weather? Have you got a dog-team?"

"Whoa! Well, let's see." Pete chewed his lip as he tried to clarify the planning of his life into a sentence or two. "Yes, I've got a team. Use 'em when I go to collect my furs and reset the traps. Beginning of the season I don't use 'em. It takes me about a month to run the line. I don't worry much about the weather; I've got six cabins along the line. Stock 'em ahead of time with a cache of food. Hole in there, if I have to.

"Ben here's been talkin' plenty about wilderness survival, I know. I can tell you this much. A trapper has to know all the tricks of survival; but he don't deliberately set out to spend the winter living on pemmican and frozen fish and sleeping in snowbanks under an improvised shelter. Makes a good story, but he don't do it!"

"Is your line ever poached on?" John questioned.

"I've heard about some bitter feuds in the North woods."

Pete chuckled. "Well, now, I've had trouble with poachers sometimes—not too much. Haven't had any for quite a spell now, not from any Crees, anyhow. I had my suspicions about certain o' them a few years ago, so I got to talkin' to them, and I told them about a horrible sight I'd seen. Just as I was about to portage around the rapids at the head of my trap line. Oh, my, it was awful! Monstrous creature, it was, with long skinny arms covered with silver hair, and it climbed out of the river and went stalkin' off through the woods—right along my line. I was sure afraid it was the Witigo. So was the Indians. Yes, sir, they was sure afraid. Had no trouble with poachers at all since then."

When our laughter had died down, he added, "Last winter I was lucky. So was everyone else in this part of the country. Had plenty of meat. Caribou."

"Caribou?" we exclaimed.

"Yes, sir. I could show you where hundreds of them trampled down the moss in back of one of my cabins. Thought I told you about that. Migration time. Don't run into that very often this far south. Caribou, yes, sir! I was kind of excited about that."

We were still sweltering with the heat late in the evening. During the day it had been 78° in the shade and 98° in the sun. The Far North is not an icebox the year around.

That night we had the worst campsite we had hit all summer. Matted solid with brush and knee-high grass, it was a mosquito-infested hole. They were there to greet us by the millions.

Head-nets and gloves offered some protection. In the fading light of late afternoon you couldn't see very well through the mesh, but if you yanked off the head-net the mosquitoes actually attacked in such swarms that you couldn't open your eyes. It wasn't a case of swatting. To be able to see and breathe it took continual brushing and mopping them off by the handful.

While the rest of the crew portaged, pitched tents, and gathered wood I was supposed to get the evening meal started. I worked frantically pulling out grass and shrubs to make a clearing large enough for a cooking fire. Arm-loads of lush grass thrown on top of my fire made a first class smudge. In jig time the clouds of insects were replaced by clouds of billowing acrid smoke wafting through camp. Smarting eyes and runny noses were preferable to being eaten alive. By replenishing one end of the fire with grass to keep the smoke rolling, and allowing the other end to burn freely for the pots and kettles, we managed to survive the onslaught.

Meanwhile our teen-agers seemed unaware of any physical miseries. They were having a hilarious time casting from shore and tossing throw lines into the swirling current to bring in one brook trout after the other until they had enough to feed thirteen hungry people. These fish were not educated to fancy tackle. They struck short but they were not at all particular. They nipped at anything that hit the water, whether it was a spoon, plug or spinner. A piece of an old sock or red handkerchief worked just as well as an expensive lure. A hand line wrapped around a stick and carried in a pocket brought in just as many as the best rods and reels. The wilderness traveler, depending on fish for food, need not be encumbered when a cigar box will hold all the equipment he needs.

Muskeg Portage around the falls came the first thing next morning. It was a dilly—three-eights of a mile through just plain swamp. We human pack horses had a sweet time getting through that moss-covered bog. In every direction stretched low brush, a few dwarfed black spruce trees and what seemed like endless spongy tussocks. With not the slightest hint of a trail and no landmarks to aim for, each man struck out for himself. There is no spring to the steps of a man burdened under more than a hundred pounds of tumped duffel. There were tussocks, but they always gave way before he could step to another one, and he would sink in halfway to his knees, bending almost double and pulling with every ounce of strength to get a foot and leg out of that gooey muck. Although rubbers worn over the moccasins fit high over the instep, now and then they were sucked off. We couldn't afford to leave such precious footgear at

Muskeg Portage. There was nothing to do but slump down, ease the tumpline load, retrieve the rubbers, reload and slug on.

A few feet below the surface there was ice that never entirely melts the year around. The ooze and slime that we sank into was freezing cold. Our feet were the only cool part of our anatomy. In spite of being lightly clothed, in anticipation of what we knew would be another hot day, we were drenched with perspiration. Mosquitoes and flies came at us, piercing through thin shirts and pants and nearly driving us mad. By the time we had crossed and re-crossed this hole three times (we were now down to three trips on a portage) nerves were jangling, tempers peevish and the language colorful.

To top it off, at the far end there was a steep bank with a sheer drop to the swirling water. With no level spot to stack the tons of dunnage, packs and boxes teetered at precarious angles all the way up the bank. There was room to float and reload only one canoe at a time. Two men hanging onto ropes tied to the bow and stern braced themselves about ten feet up the hill. A third man stood on a ledge about six inches wide and a foot under water with his legs act-ing as a cushion to keep the floating canoe from bang-ing on the rocks. A fourth man was stationed in the canoe to grab and stack boxes and packs that were re-layed down the slope.

After the portage, Pete left us to head off through the bush for some prospecting. There was a lot of respect in the voices that told him good-by. "Nothing like a trapper with a life-vest on to cure a dude's over-confidence, eh, Ben?" he said to the Chief with a wink. "What you goin' to do without me?"

"I think they're sufficiently impressed, Pete."

"You're not kidding," said Walt and Chuck and Fred in unison.

Snarkey added, "I dunno; maybe I should have studied music this summer instead."

8

Middle of Nowhere

SIZABLE STREAMS NOW TUMBLED INTO THE GOD'S River over beds of gravel, sand and small boulders. In between there were seeping, brownish trickles of melting ice from the muskeg. Gently-sloping banks rising to a height of fifteen or twenty feet were heavily forested. In the thick stands of spruce there were small groves of white birch, and here and there a tamarack and a jack pine.

An hour's paddle beyond Muskeg Portage the river suddenly narrowed to about thirty feet in width, to shoot between two high massive walls of solid granite. Known to the natives as The Gorge, it was a spectacularly beautiful spot. There was little time to gaze at the scenery and revel in its beauty. That powerful current was hurtling us precariously close to this thunderous torrent as we landed to make the portage.

Once again it was unload and tote through trailless brush with clouds of flies and mosquitoes to plague us.

Beyond The Gorge a five-mile-an-hour current swept us on our way. Clay banks rising to heights of forty to sixty feet, and so steep that they gave footing to only sparse vegetation, were eroded to form a series of pyramids with draws and gullies in between. By mid-afternoon we were approaching an extremely dangerous stretch. Between us and our next campsite there was a succession of wild rapids. The three canoes nosed in at the foot of a steep bank for a conclave. The Chief described the hazards that lay ahead and each man was assigned specific duties.

The river man knows that learning to run one rapids doesn't teach him how to run the next one. He is well aware of the tremendous changes from year to year, day to day, and even hour to hour. Each year the churning ice in the spring shoves rocks before it, gouging out new channels. Each season there are great fluctuations in water levels. When the water is very low the bars, reefs and boulders, close to the surface, make for rough going. But with less volume the currents are not as tricky and the rapids relatively tame. With a medium level, reefs and rocks are hidden, the currents faster and the rapids wilder. In high water the rapids may be ferocious and approaches to portages very dangerous. In flood conditions the whole river may be so wild and vicious that to attempt to travel would be suicidal.

With changing levels, a jagged rock lying inno-cently two feet below the surface one month may rip the bottom out of a passing canoe the next. A current that has been safe may be so powerful a week later that it can swing you broadside in a twinkling of an eye. The man who reads water knows that even wind direction can alter its behavior and that it may change from minute to minute, as a mass that seems to be moving forward suddenly returns almost like a tide.

In the first three days on the God's River our crew had found that they had come through spots so wild that it seemed as though no one in his right mind would have tackled them. On the other hand, there had been rapids that looked perfectly safe to the greenhorn but spelled portage in capital letters to the veteran. They knew, too, that this was just the be-ginning. Estuaries were pouring in from both sides; we would keep rolling downhill for the next few hun-dred miles with the river increasing daily in volume and speed.

Running these rapids started out by grabbing the branches of the shrubs along shore and bushwhacking until we came to a series of drops over rock ledges. There we resorted to lowering the canoes downstream backwards. In the stern, which had now become the nose-heavy bow, rode a lone passenger. By pulling to the right or left with powerful strokes, he could zig and zag around rocks and control the direction in-shore or offshore as necessary. To supply brakes and to keep the high-riding back end from being swept broadside of the current, a fifty-foot length of half-inch hemp rope was fastened to the plate, as in roping, and was manned from shore. Several men, keeping abreast with each canoe as it was being lowered, stood waist-deep in the eddy, and braced themselves against the force of the current. Their job was to extend their paddles to act as bumpers and prevent the canvas sides of the canoes from touching the sharp edge of the menacing rock ledge. More bushwhacking and more lining had finally brought them to a stretch of rapids that they ran until they neared a six-foot falls. At that point they unloaded and made a short lift-over at the falls.

From there on the old river swirled and roared. Near Painted Stone there were navigable chutes, but to hit them squarely demanded dexterous handling and brute manpower matched against tremendous water power. Rather than take any unnecessary chances in losing our precious supplies, Ben chose a different bowman each time, and made three trips to bring the loaded canoes through.

Orie and I, aghast, had walked to camp, to start supper for the crew. Now we watched as they reared, pitched, tossed and flew on past camp. At the end of the rapids they veered sharply and paddled upstream in the eddy to return to camp. They had come through safely with but one minor casualty. Ben was limping with a painful knee that had been badly wrenched while lining.

Painted Stone was a beautiful spot, but as a camp-site it left much to be desired. That beautiful dome of granite was an outcropping that dropped off into a dense matted thicket of waist-high brush, and we had to hack out clearings for our tents.

The fog lifted next morning, and we packed up and shoved off, in anticipation of a long hard day's travel from Painted Stone to the next campsite at Red Sucker.

An hour's paddle brought us to what is known as The Chutes. The God's River not only had narrowed again, but all its water, now crowded together, shot around a bend. There was too much river in too small a space. Wild waves rolled into a viciously curling backwash. It was all too obvious that an attempt to shoot the chutes here would end in a nose dive and swamping. Not until after we had cautiously recon-noitered on both banks could we find a safe place to land and unload to make the short but necessary carry.

At more and more frequent intervals clear, swift, gravel-bottomed streams poured in on both sides to add hour by hour and day by day to the volume and speed of current in the God's River. As we continued on a winding course, we had to be more and more careful to keep to the outside of each bend.

Crossing and recrossing a river points up the difference between map miles and canoe miles. Whether canoe cruising is by lake travel, following shore lines and dipping into deep bays, or by a river route which requires constant zigzagging, adding 25 per cent to map mileage is probably an underestimate. To cover an itinerary of around eight hundred and fifty miles we would actually paddle over a thousand.

During the fast downstream ride on the God's River I was supposed to be privileged to sit in the bottom and be relieved of part of this thousand miles of pushing. This afternoon the Chief suddenly ordered me back into harness.

"*Esox* and *Shekel* seem to have decided that it's foolish to exert themselves," he muttered, "as long as there's a five-mile current to do the work. They're too far behind. I've told them time and again we've got to follow right on each other's heels if we want to be safe. Lean on that paddle, Marion!"

When we shot so far ahead that they had to lean on *their* paddles to catch up, *Esox* and *Shekel* were roused from their lethargy.

This was another day in which we covered ground while eating lunch, by drifting with the current instead of landing. Three miles without a lick of work; peanut butter sandwiches on hardtack, and candy bars, washed down with river water.

We were approaching the dreaded Red Sucker Rapids. We could hear a thunderous roar long before we reached the Red Sucker River; and when it came into view it appeared to be almost as large as the God's, one roaring mass of white water pouring in on the right. Now instead of one wild river, there were two joining forces against us, both of them rolling downhill over outcroppings of the Canadian shield, the last granite rock between us and Hudson Bay. Rock ledges extended almost the entire width of the river. With precipitous clay banks rising now to a height of a hundred feet, portaging was impossible. The loaded canoes had to be brought through somehow.

The rapids were three miles long. For four hours the crew struggled to cover that three miles, alternately running, lining, lowering and wading.

I stood on a jutting rock point and watched John, Fred and Walt out in the madly rushing river, facing upstream and bracing themselves against the rocks. I wondered how they had strength enough to keep from being swept off their feet. With grim, set expressions, knees bent and leaning forward from the waist to help themselves withstand the force, they had nothing to hang on to except each other. I saw them balance tipsily without looking anywhere but at the canoes being roped down to them. Down came the first one; they caught it and directed it, and it was roped on past them. They stood in that precarious balance again as they watched for the next one; and then, just as it was coming through, Walt faced downstream for the instant when he reached for it, and lost his balance. The tremendous force of the water hit him from behind and took his feet out from under him. He sprawled headlong with waves washing over him. Fred made a lunge, grabbed him and hung on.

Being a good swimmer would not mean a thing if you were being bounced over drops in rock ledges in that raging current. And it took trigger-quick reactions like Fred's to keep you from it. Walt yelled "Thanks!" and they both went back to the struggle with the canoe. It was all in the day's work.

Finally all passengers climbed aboard for a fast ride through navigable chutes ahead. Paddling vigorously to make sure we were moving faster than the current, we were traveling at a breathtaking speed when suddenly Ben aimed straight for the clay bank for a forced landing. Back-paddling hard, we came in with a jolt. What we needed was air-brakes. Just before we hit, the bowman of each canoe, grabbing the painter in one hand, jumped, fell to his knees, dug in and held onto that rope for dear life as the stern, still out in the current, started to swing downstream. Had he lost his hold, the rest of his crew would have gone hurtling away.

Out in the middle of God's River, which here was perhaps a quarter of a mile wide, there was just one mean narrow chute. That was why we had come in to shore so suddenly. "Chuck and I will make three trips with the canoes, loaded, through there," Ben decided. "The rest of you walk on into camp. Marion, you get the tripod and movie camera set up. See if you can get us on film when we come through."

Clay banks receded into the background as we worked our way through waist-high meadow rue toward the large point of smooth granite rock that was to be our home for the night. Everybody gathered at a vantage point to watch for the first canoe.

"Here they come! Roll 'em, Marion!"

Through the chute—whizz! bounce!—into the five-foot rolling waves below. The canoe reared like a bucking bronco, came down hard with resounding smacks. Chuck, in the bow, shot so high out of the water that his paddle swished through thin air. They raced on past camp, veered in to shore below the white water, and paddled back to us in the eddy.

The whole crew was full of pep that evening. Three and a half weeks on the trail had hardened them so that they could take any kind of rough going in stride. For the first week or two tremendous exertion accompanied by the discomforts of trail and camp had taxed muscles and tempers and exhausted everyone both physically and mentally. But today they had worked from five in the morning until seven in the evening and had endured the grueling experience of battling the currents and wading in ice water for hours getting through Red Sucker rapids. Yet they showed no signs of exhaustion. On the contrary, routine camp chores were something to be dispensed with in nothing flat, with fish waiting to be caught in the thunderous plunging river.

Somehow Mike had managed to beat Steve in finishing his chores and had already started reeling in brook trout. Steve, in his anxiety to make up for lost time, made a dash for shore. On the slimy rock he started to slide and kept right on going. His long legs

flew through the campfire and dumped the two-gallon
kettle of macaroni and cheese into the mud.

"Gee whiz! Holy *cow!* My gosh!" he wailed.

"Well," I said philosophically, "we can't waste food
where there's none to buy. Let's wash it!"

So we scooped up the macaroni and washed it. Several dunkings left the outside looking innocently
clean. But the inside of all those hollow tubes was
filled with grit.

"Fine abrasive for our teeth!" said Art.

That was just a beginning. Steve, instead of leaving
us, gave up his fishing to help clean up the mess.
Again he slipped, this time kicking over a full canvas
bucket of water to make the mud that much muddier.
No sooner was the macaroni scooped up and once
again boiling merrily, when a gust of wind came
along, hit the reflector oven, tipped it over, and out
fell the biscuits. Raw biscuits were positively not
washable and could not be salvaged. Art had to start
all over again mixing another batch.

The heavens opened up on us before breakfast next
morning. We were stormbound. For hours we stood
around discussing all manner of subjects and at the
same time making vain attempts to dry wet clothes
by dangling them over the fire on sticks and poles.
Everyone had long since given up trying to *keep* dry
even in fair weather. You simply expect, as part of
the day's work on the trail, to jump in the river, fully
clothed, not once but many times. It is just a matter
of whether you will be in icy water to your knees,

your waist or your chin, and for how long. When every stitch of clothing you possess is soaked, you begin to dread the thought of tugging and pulling on wet clothes in the chill of early morning. When socks are wet for days or a week at a time you soon discover that the best way to handle the situation is to "wear them dry." Take them off, wring them out, and put them on again.

Yet in spite of our being chilled and wet for long periods of time, there is no such thing as catching cold. If we brought any bacteria in with us, our vigorous health and resistance had licked them. In this country there were no new germs to invade and attack us.

The Chief said, as we sat around the campfire in the evening, "Not that I think any of you need it by now—you've shaped up pretty well in these three weeks—but there's a story I'd like to tell you that'll dispel any lurking overconfidence that may be in you."

"A true story?"

"A true adventure story. You've heard me mention Karl Bayly. Well, Karl and a half-breed companion by the name of Lawrence Thomas had set out from God's Lake to explore a hundred and fifty miles into unmapped territory."

Unmapped territory—always words that meant adventure. We gathered closer to hear the tale.

"Karl and his friend were going to try to find a new route to Red Sucker Lake, where they wanted to set up a winter trading post for Indian trappers. This was in September. When they had been out for four days, snow flurries made it impossible to see far enough ahead to pick out landmarks.

"A bit puzzled as to just where they were and how far it might be to Red Sucker River, they decided to go ashore. After walking some distance to reach higher ground, Bayly climbed a tree to get a better view of the lay of the land. He saw what he thought must be Red Sucker River and sent the Indian back to get the canoe. While Thomas was gone, Karl went on inland to a higher ridge and climbed another tree. This time he slipped and fell. When he came to, faint and dazed, he found himself in strange surroundings. The area was burned over. The forested ridge where he had fallen was nowhere in sight. There was a bump on the back of his head and his left arm hung limp and useless.

"Karl had no idea of how long or how far he had wandered. All food and extra clothing were in the canoe. His pockets were empty except for a knife and six matches. Surely, he thought, he could not have come far. He started walking. For three days he walked. His only food was spruce tips, roots and rose haws. At the end of the third day he came to a strange lake. He turned back, but he was by now so weak and confused that he could no longer remember the direction from which he had come.

"On the sixth day a bad snowstorm hit. He had three matches left, and his survival depended on keeping warm. In the hollow of a fallen rotting tree he lit a fire with one of his precious matches. With his knife he worked away until he had a hole in the side of the log to provide a draft. On top of the coals he packed moss so the fire would keep smoldering. With strength ebbing he collected spruce tips, rose haws and seeds for food, then built a shelter of boughs before the fire, prepared to sit out the storm. Snow continued to fall for four days.

"On the eleventh day of his ordeal, the skies cleared. Karl started to move once again with the hope that his companion had made the trip back to God's Lake by now to get help, and that in the fresh snow he might come across the footprints of a searching party. For two more days he staggered on. Raucously-calling ravens followed him, and his one thought was that these carrion-eaters were waiting for him to die.

"Too sick and weak to go on, and with no idea of where he was or which way to go, he took the next to the last match and built a fire, totally unaware that he was within shouting distance of the Red Sucker River. An Indian passing by on the way to his trapping grounds, hugging the shore in a cold biting wind, smelled the smoke and landed to investigate. As he approached the fire he spied the emaciated, dirty white man. The huddled figure did not move. This must be work of the Witigo for sure. The frightened Indian turned and crept back to his canoe, took his gun and fired two shots to chase the evil spirit away. Roused by the gunfire, Bayly, unable to walk, dragged himself toward the sound. The Indian had already started paddling to get away from the Witigo, but as Bayly called out weakly and waved, he recognized him.

"He lifted Karl into his canoe and removed some of his own clothing to wrap around the sick man. At his camp just two miles away, he kept Karl and nursed him back to strength with fish soup.

"What of his companion? Well, Lawrence Thomas had first returned to the tree where he had left his friend. Finding him no place in sight he had called and called, with no answer. Bewildered, and then terrorized, he decided that the Witigo had done away with Karl. Back he went to God's Lake, now four sleeps away, to tell his tale. A party of searchers had set out. Two by two they had combed the area. At one time they thought they had found a trace of Karl's trail, but the heavy snows finally made further search futile.

"Knowing that the missing man had no food, no gun, and was scantily clad in the bitter cold, they felt that he must have perished. Ice was beginning to form in the bays. There was concern over the possibility that the whole party of searchers would get stranded in the freeze-up. Before starting the return trip to God's Lake, they set up a tent and left a gun and a cache of food with the faint hope that Karl might be alive and find them.

"Karl Bayly was a master woodsman. If he had not

lost consciousness in his fall, he would have been perfectly capable of finding his way and subsisting. The near tragedy, in this instance, had not been due to incompetence."

Ben ended his story: "Any man who uses common sense, keeps his wits about him, and travels cautiously to avoid accidents, can survive for long periods in the bush country merely by having with him at all times a few items of equipment so simple and so light that he can carry them in his pockets. Waterproof matches, a pocket knife, snare wire and a slingshot for killing small game, a hand line for catching fish, and some salt."

Steve said thoughtfully, "We aren't even roughing it, are we? We're living like kings. It sure gives you something to think about."

9

Top of the World—Almost

ON THE TWENTIETH OF JULY, A FIVE O'CLOCK RISING call put us off for an early start to cover the 60 miles between Red Sucker and the trading post at Shamattawa in one day's run. Twenty-five days on the trail had brought us to the halfway mark in time but not in distance. We were still a 180 miles from York Factory. To reach the Bay and return to our starting point at Norway House we had 650 miles to go in the next 25 days.

Coursing between hundred-foot clay banks, the God's River now changed direction from east to north. Though the weather was sunny, a brisk head wind chilled us to the marrow and reminded us that, as the crow flies, we were not far from the ocean.

Suddenly the Chief pointed to some scrubby second-growth timber. "See that? It's starting to cover the scars of a forest fire that swept through here in 1940. Do you know—you won't believe it—but since the discovery of gold in the 1930's, many fires have been set deliberately, by prospectors, to make their search for riches easier! In order to find out what the earth's crust had to offer, they simply denuded the surface. I'd like to wring the necks of 'em all. Personally!"

Hour by hour the topography was changing, gradually but steadily. We were obviously almost into the true Far North—the sub-Arctic. The banks now were not so high, and clay had given way to sand and coarse gravel. During the afternoon we began to see the first signs of the great belt of limestone that surrounds Hudson Bay. At first there were scattered small patches. Later we found ourselves rolling downhill through fast shallow water that flowed over solid, light-colored shelves as we approached the junction of the God's and the Echoing rivers. Echoing River was just as rolling, just as fast, and here where they came together, appeared to be the wider of the two. Where it pours into the God's, it looks as large as the Mississippi at most points, and it drains a vast area. Yet very few people have ever heard of it, or of countless rivers of the Far North.

Straight ahead of us, on a ten-foot bank, was Shamattawa, which in the Cree language means "meeting of rivers." A small store and a few scattered cabins comprise the settlement at this Hudson's Bay Company outpost, boarded up and completely deserted now, with not even a barking sled-dog to greet us.

"Treaty Week," said Ben. "They've all gone to York Factory for their annual get-together."

We shoved on in search of a campsite, though we had already covered the sixty miles which had sounded like an overambitious goal for one day.

The hop from Shamattawa to York Factory—one hundred and twenty miles—could have been made nonstop, and would have been under different circumstances. But our botanists had work to do here. This was a transition zone between the solid granite rock of the ancient Pre-Cambrian shield and the limestone belt. This change was of great importance, biologically speaking, and required time out for extensive plant collecting. John and Orie would have to comb the area for all types of specimens, and this would keep us in the vicinity for several days.

The river, here half a mile wide, flowed swiftly over a solid limestone shelf. But on the shores the change was not so clear-cut for there was no striking difference in tree growth. Among the plants there were many entirely new varieties mixed with those we had been seeing all along our route.

"Look! Violets! On the twenty-first of July!" shouted someone.

We were following spring northward.

Hugging the right-hand shore we passed markers of Indian graves and a few pole frames that had been used for tepees. We were on the canoe route over which supplies are brought from York Factory to the Shamattawa trading post; at any moment we expected to see smoke curling from a campfire and come upon our first sight of other human beings since we had left God's Lake ten days before.

Instead, we found that neither the Indians nor the Ferriers could possibly pitch a tent on banks that became not only precipitous but rose to heights of eighty to a hundred feet. This was a predicament. We were nearing Limestone Rapids. The opposite shore looked promising, but the river was wide and very fast. We had no choice but to cross. Even though we angled the bows upstream and paddled like demons, we steadily lost ground and landed far below the point aimed for.

Not until after we went ashore to look around did we discover that we had accidentally come upon a large and frequently used campsite. Judging by the rubbish scattered about, Indians had been there within the past few days. Cached in the shrubs was a canoe. Hurrying to clean up and burn a collection of trash, I picked up a six-page mimeographed pamphlet, *The Cree Monthly Guide.*

The first bit of reading material I had seen in many weeks was fascinating, even though I was left almost completely in the dark as to its contents. The heading on each of the six pages was in English, but the script

was a series of unconnected symbols. From the head-
ings, I made out that this was a bulletin put out by a
church mission. The guidance was not only spiritual
in nature but also educational, for interspersed here
and there were English words for which there was
evidently no counterpart in the Indian vocabulary.
Words such as penicillin, streptomycin, sulpha drugs,
bubonic plague, typhoid fever and cholera. Could it
be possible that the last three indicated that in this
day and age these diseases were still rampant?

From our contacts with these northern Indians we
knew that few of them speak our language. Though
there have been attempts made by various churches
and the Indian Service to educate the children, it has
been slow and often discouraging. These people continue innately primitive. There are no villages as
such. Even though a few families may gather around
a mission or trading-post settlement for the few short
summer months, fall finds them heading for their
trap lines. A teacher, if there is one, may wake up to
find all his pupils gone, not to be seen again until
spring, except for the few whose fathers are perma-
nently employed at the post.

For the written language the Crees are indebted
to James Evans, a preacher and printer, who was sent
into the North in 1840 as a Methodist missionary. As
other men in America have done for other Indian
nations, he set about to bring the written word to a
spoken language. Instead of using the Roman alpha-
bet, he made the Cree language much simpler by the

use of characters—resembling the Greek letters—
which represent not a single letter but any one of
several syllables, depending on the position of the
character. For instance: ∨, ∧, >, <, represent the
sounds "pa," "pe," "po" and "pi."

Early that afternoon we spied figures moving upstream along the opposite shore. At first they were
too far away for us to make out how many there were
or what they were doing. It turned out to be a sight
that held us fascinated for hours. The Indians were
returning from York Factory, bringing with them
the supplies for the trading post at Shamattawa. We
watched them through binoculars. On shore and at
spaced intervals, there were clusters of men as far as
we could see. Out in the river was a string of some
strange manner of craft, obviously much larger than
canoes.

Finally it dawned on us. The one hundred and
twenty miles from the Bay was a continuous river
route requiring no portages. What we saw was a
whole string of barges. On the long tracking rope attached to each barge there were six to eight men en-
gaging in a tug-of-war against the forces of the God's
River. The bank was so steep, the footing so poor and
the current so swift that at times they fell to their
knees.

Progress was so slow that it was hours before they
came close enough for us to be able to hear their
voices. They were singing, and the songs ended in a
burst of hilarious shouting. At any moment we ex-

pected to hear the strains of "The Volga Boatmen."

It is generally conceded that the Indian is not over-endowed with ambition. Work is something to be shunned whenever possible. But this excursion to York and return is a communal affair, a time of festivity, a contest, a vying to display prowess. Each year they attempt to break old records. We learned some time later that the group we saw had covered the one hundred and twenty miles in five days. It was almost incredible, for we had watched them struggle foot by foot, advancing not more than a mile an hour. Even though there were some less difficult stretches, to average twenty-four miles a day must have meant traveling very nearly around the clock with precious little time out for sleeping or eating.

Here was a page from the history of the fur trade; the barges were merely a substitution for the canoe brigade and a crew of packers. Mechanized transportation is sounding the death knell to the old methods —we have seen the outboard motor, the airplane and the tractor train delivering supplies to the inland posts—the primitive means of travel is dying.

John and Orie and I began to remark on the similarity of the plants in this country to those found high in the mountains of western United States. There were many more similar ecological changes on the trail now. Whether you are going higher in latitude or higher in altitude, there is a like succession of altering climatic conditions, and we thought it wasn't unreasonable to expect that the environment for plant growth here, just below tree line in the Hudsonian Zone, was similar to that just below tree line on a peak in California.

There was another curious thing. Imbedded in the rock on the limestone shelf abutting the Hayes River were many fossilized shells. But we were at least two hundred and fifty feet above sea level. How did these relics of marine animals get here?

Our scientists looked at me with the same pity that Ben showed when I questioned the three of them. It was simple. The whole limestone belt fringing Hudson Bay had once been the floor of the ocean. The marine animals ingested the lime washed into the sea by the great rivers. The organic limestone that had once been the bed of the sea was now the solid rock on which we were walking.

Limestone Rapids—shallow water rushing crazily down steps of solid limestone, a rapids half a mile wide and over two miles long was the king of them all. But we were going to run it.

"Run *that?*" Frederic took one look and turned to Ben, astounded.

"He's high-strung enough as it is," volunteered Snarkey. "I could get to be high-strung myself, running that."

"But his reactions are quick, and so are yours. And

that goes for all of you," said the Chief. "There's no reason why we can't run it. The middlemen will have to stay out and walk, to lighten the load, but once that's done, there's nothing to worry about. Except doing as you know by now you have to do!"

Mike almost whispered, "How fast is it?"

"Taking our paddles into account, too, we'll be going twelve to fifteen miles an hour."

"Gee! God's River really throws 'em at you!"

I was the only middleman who rode; my hundred pounds was considered negligible. But once started, I wished fervently that my feet were on land. That ride was so wild that I just hung on and waited for the crash. There was no rhyme or reason to the behavior of the water. It ran in all directions. We slid over a shelf of limestone so dangerously close to the surface that it seemed we must be missing it by an inch. Then the wash curled over backward in gigantic waves and enveloped us in spray. Just for a second the canoe seemed to be on the bottom and the river above us. Then the stern came down with a smack and the bow leaped high out of the water.

The limestone began to break up into fine pebble-sized pieces that formed a shifting bed. As we slid through the shallows the movement of the canoes caused "sand waves," unpredictable changes in water behavior due to the motion of the river bed. A channel would disappear before we reached it; there was nothing to do but battle the currents and keep the nose straight. If we had turned sideways we would have rolled like a log over a spillway. Blocks of broken limestone with knifelike edges filled the rapids. Had we so much as touched them they would have torn our craft to ribbons.

No stretch of river ever seemed so long. But we came through without a scratch—all three canoes.

The shore line was changing again. Between the river and the imposing hundred-foot banks in the far background there was bench land of granite boulders, gravel and sand. Timber was sparse and small. The largest of the white birch were scarcely big enough for tent poles. We were very close to Hudson Bay; and the Chief announced that we would go through nonstop. Between forty and fifty miles could be covered by floating during the night. The object of the ordeal was to make up time and help keep to schedule. If everything went well we would reach Hudson Bay by noon the next day.

Until nine o'clock that evening we paddled on, then pulled in to shore to make preparations for the float. Taking turns on two-hour shifts, one man in each canoe was to be left on duty in the stern to rudder, keep on course, and be on the lookout for trouble. By stacking all gear as far to the rear as possible, the rearrangement supposedly left enough room forward for the other three to stretch out on the bottom and sleep between shifts. It would be at least two more hours before we were beyond the last of the reefs and the fast, tricky water. After that there would be a relatively safe, deep channel.

By ten o'clock it was beginning to get dark. At eleven we reached the confluence of the God's River and the Hayes, and the temperature was dropping rapidly from the low forties of the daylight hours. Where the rivers joined, Ben waited for the other two canoes to come alongside so he could give out instructions to the three men taking over at the end of the first shift.

"From here on, we'll have to follow closely in line. Keep from a hundred to three hundred feet from the left-hand shore. There are reefs and bars to the right. No talking except to wake the next man for duty. You'll have to listen for sounds that might mean trouble. If you hear riffles or rolling water, shy away from them. When you change positions, use the utmost caution to keep balance on an even keel. The man at the helm is to stick his paddle down frequently to probe for depth. The *Chief* will use a flashlight as a blinker to follow. It's going to be cold. All pawing in packs for extra jackets and gloves is to be done now while we're all together. O.K.?"

"O.K., Chief!"

Drifting through a misty, silent darkness was a ghostly experience. "Hey, the Northern Lights!" went a whisper from craft to craft. And there they were—flickering, waving, arcing over us. In midsummer the northern nights are short; we had never before been awake during this hour or two of darkness to watch the display. By two o'clock of this night daybreak had blotted it out. By three the sun was well up over the horizon.

Daylight revealed the growing immensity of the Hayes, which has the reputation of having one of the fastest currents of all the large rivers in North America. The banks were now about seventy-five feet high. The timber was scrubby and stunted. A moose watched us from the shore; we passed another one swimming. At five o'clock we came to the Pennycutaway River; without paddling a stroke we had made forty miles in six hours.

The great Hayes River was racing on the last lap of its dash to the sea. And so were we. The spirit of excitement in the *Chief,* the *Esox* and the *Shekel* was running high. The combination of swinging paddles and swift current now had added to it the force of the outgoing tide. We were rapidly approaching high-tide mark; fast water rolled over a bed of solid limestone. Banks became lower and farther and farther apart; the Hayes widened and formed a delta dotted with green islands. We dipped our fingers over the side, and tasted. It was salt water.

We wound around a curve and saw nothingness on the horizon.

"There it is!" Steve exclaimed; and Mike sounded struck with awe at what he had accomplished.

"The ocean! By George, I've paddled clear to the sea!"

Just at noon we rounded a point of land, and there

was York Factory perched atop a twenty-five-foot bank on the desolate, lonely, windswept coastline of Hudson Bay.

Thirty days after leaving Norway House we had arrived at 57° North. We had come over some of the same routes and by the same primitive means that had been used for centuries in the fur trade. We were landing near the very spot which had once been the destination of sailing ships from Europe that crossed the North Atlantic and came through Hudson Straits; from this spot men had embarked to push up the Hayes or the Nelson and probe the vast wilderness to establish colonies.

"Marion," said Ben, "I wouldn't be surprised if you're the first white woman to come down the God's to York Factory *twice*."

The boys looked surprised and questioned us.

"Five years ago when we arrived here, we learned that Marion was the first white woman ever to come down the God's River," Ben explained.

"It was quite a thrill," I added. "Sort of gives me a place in history that I thought had disappeared long ago."

York Factory is so inaccessible that the arrival of visitors is always something of an event. Once again the moccasin telegraph had been at work, and this time there were a hundred Indians lined up to watch us paddle in. We passed their cluster of shacks and tents, where small children clung to their mothers' skirts and stared as solemnly at us as their fathers stared; and some mangy sled-dogs at tether strained at their chains and yowled.

The Chief went off to the Hudson's Bay Company to ask permission to camp on the Company's grounds. Here, as at each post visited, the Company's manager, his family and employees greeted us with cordiality and graciousness and went all out to see that our needs were met. The botanists streaked off to have a look at the land, even though it appeared to be nothing but a mosquito-infested hole; the boys dispensed entirely with such mundane chores as getting lunch and pitching tents. They scattered in all directions— toward the Indian village, the Anglican mission, the Company's headquarters, the promontory—and the boardwalks sounded to the thump of their feet.

"Keep to the walks," I called after them. "This whole place is a bog in the summer." Seepage from the melting perma-ice turns every low spot into a marsh in warm weather here, for this ice lies close to the surface.

In the Company warehouse the storerooms were stacked high with goods to be sent to the outposts, but York's own supplies were startlingly low. "It's Treaty Week, you know," the manager told us, "and every Indian in the country must be spending all his money at once, I think. As usual!"

There would be another ship in with supplies before the summer was over, he said. "Three schooners every summer; and every time one comes in it's a big day. Excitement, I mean."

There were no souvenirs to buy, because there were so seldom any visitors to want them. And as for mail, well, it would be useless to try to send any from here. It might not go out for months. Nor were there any letters waiting for us. This was a world apart!

An aura of its romantic history still clings to York Factory. In 1670 Charles II granted a charter to "The Governor and Company of Adventurers of England Trading into Hudson Bay," giving them the sole rights to carry on the fur trade in northern Canada. It goes without saying that those rights would not be unchallenged. Within a few years after the granting of the charter, York was one of several forts that were established on the coast of Hudson Bay and James Bay. These forts were raided, captured, surrendered and recaptured many times in the next hundred and ten years of rivalry for control of this lucrative trade. The Company continued to expand and grow in strength, overcame the hostility of the Indians, and drove out the French, only to be plagued by rival groups of British traders. Finally in 1821 the Hudson's Bay Company and the Northwest Company merged. This brought peace and the end of serious competition.

In the heyday of the great fur trade, it was from here that the twenty-five to thirty-foot York boats embarked. A colorful sight it must have been when a crew of around a hundred manning a brigade of fifteen to twenty of these weighty, cumbersome craft, left York with supplies for the inland posts hundreds of miles away, and returned laden with bales of pelts to be shipped to England and the fur markets of the world. Rowed and sailed through navigable waters, tracked upstream with ropes and pushed over portages on log rollers, these huge wooden boats had somehow been over the same route that had posed so many problems for the Ferrier party with its comparatively light canvas canoes.

At York today, Treaty Week is more to the Crees than a time for collecting the government money. It is a time of festivity, and the one week of the year when the tribe comes together. Moose feasts, soccer games, wrestling, all have their places. It is a great time for weddings. For the Royal Canadian Mounted Police, it is a good time to check up and set records in order.

At supper time our camp was full of talk about everything the crew had seen.

"Did you know some of these Company buildings are the same ones that were built around 1840? Nothing's been done to them since. Absolutely original state."

"I didn't know they'd be so big. I guess I didn't know the fur trade was so big!"

"The Mounty told me that Caribou stay north of the tree line in the summer. For the winter they migrate south in great herds to seek the shelter of the forests."

"Well, but did *you* know that they see polar bears around here from December to April! They come in off the ice to have their families inland, and then they take the cubs back to the ice."

While we were eating, the Indians' sled-dogs came skulking around our tents, growling and sniffing and making themselves obnoxious. They were no better cared for than stray mongrels.

"The Crees seem to figure there's no sense in feeding dogs during the summer when they aren't of any use," Ben said. "They're given just enough food to keep them alive, and then fattened up when the time comes for them to work."

"Gee whiz! No wonder they're so mangy and ragged. And snarling. I'd be mad, too."

The dogs had been so mistreated that they did not approach within kicking distance of us, but they would not stop slinking around. Art had taken advantage of the 75° sunshine to set a big batch of yeast bread and buns to rise, and then, instead of enjoying his visit at the post, he spent most of the afternoon guarding the dough. The dogs had their eyes on it.

By the time we had finished supper one sick animal that had dragged himself near our campfire was too weak to move. We asked the natives to get their ailing dog out of our sight. They disposed of him simply—by throwing him over the steep bank.

10

The Tides of Hudson Bay

JULY 26 MARKED AN END AND A BEGINNING. THIS WAS the day that would see us homeward bound, starting the long trip back to Norway House by way of the mighty Nelson River. Our schedule gave us only 20 days to cover approximately 500 miles. A paddle of 120 miles from York would bring us to the tracks of Churchill railroad where we would board a train, travel 166 miles by rail, and put into the Nelson again at Thicket Portage.

The saying that what goes up must come down may be a scientific truism. But for us it was reversed to what comes down must go up. For over a month we had been traveling down north through a country where there is more water than there is land and where the waterways are the only highways. As the rivers increased steadily in volume, size, and speed, and dropped to seek the ocean level, the current had pushed us faster and faster until the climax had been reached when it was possible to travel the last hundred and twenty miles from Shamattawa to York in one day.

To return to our starting point meant battling our way back upstream, meeting head on the force of the current of a river that drains half a continent. The hundred and twenty miles from York up the Nelson River to the railroad was to take us not a day but a week of doggedly hard work that called for a whole new set of techniques and skills of canoemanship. But before we could actually turn our noses southward we had to reach the mouth of the Nelson.

At York a point of low-lying land extends for five miles out into Hudson Bay. On both sides of Marsh Point and far out beyond its tip there are shoals which, combined with the shifting tides, make travel near shore impossible. The tides of this section of Hudson Bay rank close to the highest in the world, and the distance from high tide mark to low tide mark ranges from five to ten miles. To round the point we had to head out into ocean waters, miles from shore. From the time we left York until we reached the nearest available campsite on the Nelson River thirty miles away, we would be at the mercy of the tides. There would be no possibility of making a landing or turning back, regardless of what happened.

The white man, even though he may be possessed

of scientific knowledge and a theoretical understanding of tidal action, cannot compete with the native when it comes to practical application. What the Indians at York had to say about all the dangers of canoe travel on the ocean was not very comforting. Under the most ideal of conditions the time element posed serious problems.

We would, they said, have to leave York at exactly the crucial moment when the tide was halfway out. A five-mile paddle would bring us even with the tip of Marsh Point. But we would have to paddle to a guide post another five miles out beyond the point to catch the next incoming tide that would carry us up into the mouth of the Nelson River. Beyond this marker we must not go.

If we reached the marker ahead of time we would have to stick our paddles down in the mud, hold the canoes, let the tide go out from under us, and wait for the incoming tide. If we left York too early, the outgoing tide would be too fast and the water too deep for us to anchor and hold the canoes at the guidepost, and we would be carried miles too far out in the ocean. If we left York too late, the tide would sweep out ahead of us and leave us stranded on the mud flats before we reached the marker. That would leave us in the predicament of having the incoming tide sweep us back where we came from.

Assuming that we left York at the most propitious moment, we would have two hours to make the ten miles to the guidepost and four hours to cover the remaining twenty miles to camp before the tide started working against us to push us back out in the ocean. That meant swinging the paddles as hard and as fast as we could swing for six straight hours without a break in order to average five miles an hour. Even though everything went smoothly it would be an endurance contest.

Unfortunately, in preparing for all eventualities, the timing was only one element. The Indians told us that there were very few days when weather conditions were such that, in rounding the point by canoe, they did not run into complications of one sort or another. It was not the briny deep but the shallowness of the boulder-strewn mud flats that made it dangerous unless you were blessed with a calm sea all the way. In the shallows a wind kicks up short choppy waves that could pick you up and bounce you down smack on top of a rock. A head wind so slows progress that you cannot keep up with the receding tide and are left stranded on the flats, miles from shore, with no place to go for shelter. The situation is really grave if, while you are sitting it out on the floor of the ocean, a sudden fierce storm sweeps in and the next incoming tide bears down on you in the form of five-foot rollers that could either wash over you, swamping the canoe, or pick it up and let it down on a boulder with a crash, smashing it to smithereens.

By prearrangement, two of the natives were on hand to give us the go signal on the morning we left York Factory. At three o'clock we piled out of our sleeping bags. Nobody had slept very soundly. We were all thinking too much of what lay ahead. By five o'clock we had broken camp, carried our gear out across the flats left by the steadily receding tide, were loaded and standing kneedeep in water alongside the canoes to keep them afloat. At five-thirty the Indians waved us off. The time was right. They saw no signs of stormy weather. The sea was calm.

For an hour we pushed rhythmically and steadily through the opaque, ugly-looking salt water, confident that everything was going well. Then suddenly we found ourselves bucking a head wind. Because of it we were twenty-five minutes late in reaching the ten-mile marker. The *Shekel* had managed to keep pace with our lead canoe, but the *Esox* was lagging far behind, too far for safety. It was time to turn to head into the mouth of the Nelson River. With the wind now at our backs we might still have been able to make it by putting on an extra spurt. But we dared not get too far ahead of the *Esox*. Our only choice was to slow down. By the time they caught up to us and all three canoes were once more together, we were fifty minutes behind schedule. Walt had dropped his wallet overboard and they had taken time to try to fish it out.

That did it! The tide swept out from under us. We were grounded. In all directions there were nothing but mud flats. The nearest campsite was five miles away. It would be eight hours before the incoming tide returned to put us afloat, and there wasn't a thing we could do but sit and wait for it. The crew made light of the situation. This was a lark they hadn't planned on.

The final words when we pushed off from York had been that for the next thirty miles everyone was to lean on those paddles without missing a stroke. Regardless of how tired or hungry we were there was to be no time out for rest or nourishment until we were safely in camp. This was a good joke on the Chief. Right in the middle of what was supposed to be an endurance contest, we had eight hours to rest, with the floor of the ocean for a picnic grounds.

Their only worry seemed to be that there was no wood for building a cooking fire and no drinking water within miles. If they had to go hungry and thirsty this wouldn't be so much fun after all. From the lead canoe came kettles of fresh water. Anticipating a long day of sea travel, we had had the forethought to fill them and stow them aboard before we left York. Art brought out the cinnamon rolls that he had laboriously baked the previous afternoon, and Ben dug into the supply of candy. "What a life! No dishes to wash, either!" chortled Franklin.

One of the boys said, "I read in a book once about a kid who was able to wander around on the bed of the ocean!" And off they all went to do the same.

Then the sky that had been bright all morning became overcast and ugly. The barometer was falling.

At six o'clock, as the tide started creeping toward us inch by inch, each four-man crew stood by, holding the bows pointed upstream. A chilling wind that blew directly off the floating drift ice out in the Bay and the cold water lapping deeper and deeper on our legs had us all shivering. As soon as the canoes were floated freely we gave a push, hopped in and paddled on. The mouth of the Nelson River where it pours into the Bay is eight to ten miles wide, the bed filled with rocks carried downstream by the current and the churning ice of the spring thaws. The force of the incoming tide swept us on over the rocky shallows as we angled in toward the left bank of the river.

Suddenly the sky turned black. A cold northwest wind came howling in off the ocean with gale force. Lightning flashed and thunder crashed. The clouds opened up and the rain came in sheets. Tide water that had been rolling gently a few minutes before now kicked up into waves so choppy that it was impossible to ride the crests. We bounced up and over, then down into a trough, praying that we would not hit bottom.

Our one thought was to reach shore and safety. We were still a good two miles from camp, and the shore line for which we headed was nothing but a low flat marsh that was gradually being covered by the seeping salt water. In the rain and darkness we could not see more than a few feet ahead of us, but we made tracks for that swamp and didn't stop until the reeds and brush allowed us to go no farther. Kneedeep water lapped around us, but at least we were safely out of the chaotic waves.

With that bone-chilling wind coming straight off the Arctic ice-fields, we shook with the cold and wrung the sea-water from ourselves as best we could. We could not reach dry land. We dared not head out again into the rough water. If we stayed where we were for the night, the tide would eventually go out and leave us stranded again.

At the end of a half-hour Ben made up his mind that the combination of fatigue, cold, exposure and inactivity might have dire results and that we must keep moving. The order went out to start wading and pushing the canoes through the reeds and brush in the direction of camp. The downpour changed to a drizzle and we could now see the outline of a rising shore line ahead. We waded out of the marsh and were forced to hop in and paddle across a stretch of rough water. A small fresh-water creek and a bank covered with stunted spruce meant camp. To lighten the loads and bring the canoes safely through the shallows of the last fifty feet, we waded ashore, stumbling through the darkness. At last we planted our feet on the first piece of dry ground we had seen since leaving York Factory.

In a howling wind and another torrential downpour, everyone raced to get gear unloaded and tents pitched. Though we had planned to seek protection from the storm in the scrubby growth of timber on the twenty-foot bank, we were too exhausted to make the climb. The gravel beach just beyond high tide mark had to be our home for the night. As soon as we landed, millions of mosquitoes attacked us. The beams of flashlights revealed clouds of the demons. The pelting rain made repellents useless. In a matter of minutes, faces, hands, and the tops of our heads were covered with itching welts.

Miserably cold, wet and weary we dove into tents, peeled off our sopping clothes and crawled into sleeping bags. No mention was made of food. We went to bed hungry, thankful to be safely ashore.

All night and all the following day the storm raged on. The tents whipped in the gale, and the canvas snapped and cracked like rifle shots. In the morning, when a bedraggled crew piled out, it was discovered that I was not the only one who had been expecting our shelters to be picked up and blown away or torn to shreds. For the third night in a row there had been very little sleep. No one objected to being windbound. We were sadly in need of a day's rest before tackling the Nelson.

The fierce biting wind was not conducive to hanging around camp. We spent most of the day on the move to keep warm, taking long walks along the shore, exploring, watching the ebb and flow of the tide and gazing with awe at the immensity of the river which to us was the road that led to home. Vistas in every direction were almost entirely barren, bleak and desolate. To the right of camp the delta of the Nelson spread out to become a retreating horizon of sea and sky. Outlined against the gray sky was the hull of a wrecked ship which had run aground years before. Here, where we stood, the mouth of the river was five miles wide. On the far shore and directly across from us was Port Nelson, with its huge steel network sticking out into the river —a ghost of a plan that never reached fruition. At one time this had been chosen as the site for the terminal of a railroad. The rails were to be laid from Winnipeg to Port Nelson on Hudson Bay for the purpose of shipping wheat from central Canada to England over a route that would be a thousand miles shorter than those going through the eastern seaboard ports.

But there was too little protection here from the fierce Arctic storms and it was impossible to keep open the channel dredged through tidal flats. The best engineers on earth couldn't do it. Eventually the railroad was built, but the terminus was changed to Fort Churchill.

Our maps showed that we were very near the limit of tree line. Twenty miles to the north marked the beginning of the Barren Lands. What little vegetation there was at the mouth of the Nelson was scrubby and stunted. Wildlife appeared to be scarce. A few ravens and herring gulls were the only birds we saw until late in the afternoon when we came upon a beautiful specimen of an Arctic horned owl which we added to our collection for the Iowa Museum. Everywhere there were small fossils and skeletal remains of whales. Unfortunately, these were too large to bring home for souvenirs.

Toward evening there was a promise of clearing

weather that would permit us to start battling our way upstream.

The Nelson, though it is so little known that the average American has never heard of it, ranks high among the great rivers of the world in quantity of water carried. The water pouring past our campsite had come all the way from the eastern slopes of the Canadian Rocky Mountains, through the provinces of Alberta and Saskatchewan by way of the Saskatchewan River to Lake Winnipeg and thence northeast to Hudson Bay. Tributaries all along the seventeen-hundred-mile route had added their contributions. And what has come from the west is only part of the story. The Red River of Minnesota and the whole Rainy River watershed stretching along the U.S.-Canadian boundary almost to Lake Superior, and the English River watershed around Sioux Lookout— all these drain into Lake Winnipeg, flow into the Nelson, and on to Hudson Bay.

The Nelson, unlike most large rivers, is not navigable except by canoe. For the next nineteen days we would be pointing our bows upstream into its waters. *Upstream!*

The next morning we were up at five. Once again we were at the mercy of the tide. In low tide the mud flats extended a mile or more out from shore. Had we waited for the incoming tide to cover the flats completely, we would have found ourselves with the ebb flow working against us in a few hours. Its force combined with the Nelson's would .top us dead in our tracks or push us backward. In this race against time it was necessary to meet the tide part way. We carried gear and canoes out over the flats for a few hundred feet, and sank to our ankles in the muck with every step. Canoes loaded, we stood along-side, and as the salt water began seeping in and then lapping around our feet, Ben explained once again why every minute of the next few hours would be precious. To take advantage of the tide we must put power behind every stroke with no time out to rest.

"We'll push off as soon as we can float," Ben said.

And a short while later Mike announced, scram-bling into his place and grabbing a paddle, "Now I know. Kneedeep water will float a canoe."

Our immediate goal was the opposite shore, five miles distant. For about ten minutes everything went well. Then suddenly, a north wind that had been just a breeze turned into a blow. In no time we were caught in choppy waves. For a moment Ben consid-ered turning back, but he decided that the waves might be a combination of wind and shallows. In that case, the farther out we went the deeper the water would become and the choppy sea should tone down.

That was wishful thinking. What had started out as waves became rollers seven feet high, aiming straight for us. To keep from swamping we angled into them as we pitched up over a crest and down into a trough. Everything we had went into each stroke. We wondered if we were gaining an inch. With the wind blowing upstream meeting the downstream current of the Nelson, we were caught in the midst of chaos.

To add to our worries the *Esox* and the *Shekel* were lagging farther and farther behind. In this wild rough sea we could not stop to wait for them. An empty canoe would ride the rollers, but we had too narrow a margin of buoyancy. Either we kept moving or we took the risk of being rolled or having a wall of water wash over us. But what was the matter with the other canoes? Was someone ill? Or were they so frightened that they couldn't paddle? For the time being, all Ben could do was glance back frequently to make sure they were still coming. At times they disappeared completely in the troughs of the waves.

About midway across, when we were a good two miles from either shore, we ran smack into a school of white whales. By the dozens they were coming in with the tide to feed at the mouth of the river. As they surfaced, their glistening backs appeared to be whitecaps. But the whitecaps were moving in the wrong direction and throwing up spouts!

There were no traffic signals out in the middle of the Nelson River. The whales were bent on getting upstream and we were just as bent on reaching the opposite shore. Our paths crossed. Though we were the intruders and definitely in the minority, we were in no position at the moment to yield the right of way.

At first, while they were still at some distance, we could view the spectacle with fascination and without uneasiness. It seemed a pity to be denied the opportunity of recording this high adventure on motion picture film. Camera equipment was buried deep to make sure it would not get wet during the crossing. If we took time out and stopped paddling we stood a good chance of swamping. The risk was too great, especially when we realized that on the screen the animals would probably appear only as momentary flashes indistinguishable from the whitecaps.

Meeting up with whales in the mouth of the Nelson is inevitable. Ben had had the experience many times. There was slight consolation in the fact that he had never heard of an instance in which one of them had surfaced under a canoe and upset it. There was no way to get where we were going except to pass right through the middle of the school. By the time we were surrounded on all sides and one huge body more than twelve feet long arched up so close that we could almost reach out and slap it with a paddle, we fervently hoped that the whales were just as anxious to avoid us as we were to avoid them.

Playing tag with a school of whales was a thrill in retrospect. But this was a game we were only too glad to have end as we left them in our wake and came out of the waves into the lee of the right-hand shore. Five miles in two and a half hours.

Once out of the rough water, the going was much easier. We nosed directly upstream with the force of the incoming tide in our favor. Aching arms and backs protested, but for another two hours we swung the paddles steadily until we reached Seal Island, which marks the head of the tide.

11

You Pull the Canoes Upstream

THE REST OF THE CREW CAME DRAGGING IN, HAZY about what had delayed them: waves—whales—unsteady horsepower. Yes, maybe it was cut down by fright; but they were ready to dare us to criticize them for that! In spite of their best efforts to keep up with us, the lead canoe had just pulled away from them.

"And sometimes," said Art, "you disappeared completely in the troughs of those waves and the only way we could follow your course was to watch for the top of the Chief's hat."

"And it didn't bob up very often," finished Walt.

Twenty of the ninety miles from Port Nelson to the Churchill railroad were behind us now. Beyond tidewater we came face to face with the full force of the Nelson River. The river had narrowed to a mile in width to course between fifty- to seventy-foot banks at a speed of seven miles an hour. In the seventy miles from here to the railroad, the Nelson rolled downhill from an elevation of around a hundred and eighty feet to sea level where we sat having our lunch. Uphill travel called for a whole new set of skills.

Much of the next seventy miles would be covered by hoofing it, walking along shore to pull the canoes upstream with ropes, against the force of the current. The reason for crossing from our campsite to the Port Nelson side was now obvious. The sun hit this north bank, drying it to some extent. The shaded south bank would have been impassably wet and slippery. Also on this shore there were more points of land jutting out to afford protection from the direct flow of the current.

Just as we had seen the Indians tracking up the God's River from York to Shamattawa, we would track up the Nelson. Tracking lines, three-hundred-foot lengths of quarter-inch linen rope, were brought out for the first time. A half-hour's briefing prepared the crew for the initiation.

On each canoe, one end of the rope was tied to the back thwart with a canoe knot. Its length was then strung forward and brought out from under the front thwart about three feet behind the bow. This would allow the current to swing the bow out slightly and angle the canoe upstream rather than nosing into the bank by a direct inshore pull.

One man, left on duty in the stern, had the responsibility of directing course around all obstacles by a combination of ruddering, wading, and letting out or hauling in rope. The tracking line gave him almost three hundred feet of leeway to follow the shore closely or to go out around rocks, reefs, slides, windfalls, or whatever happened to be in his path.

Attached to the shore end of each rope was a harness for the unfortunate man who did the pulling. It was fashioned from a tumpline. The three-inch-wide head strap lay diagonally across his chest. One thong passed up over a shoulder and the other under the opposite arm. Regardless of how rough the going might be, it was up to the tracker to keep moving. Under no circumstances was he to allow a slack in the line. Losing forward momentum could be disastrous. If the line were not kept taut, the canoe, swept out in the raging current, would be out of control going downstream sidewise, the rope tangled in the brush or cut by sawing on a rock. In all probability the canoe would swamp with the loss of all possessions.

Keep the rope taut and out of the water. Don't stop for anything. The instructions took on meaning almost immediately. Except for one helmsman in each canoe, the rest of us started plodding. That left two extra members of each crew on hand to help the man on the rope if he ran into trouble. For the next two hours the troubles came thick and fast.

The first hazard was a long stretch of low flat marsh. Grass, waist-high, completely hid the pitfalls of mud, slimy rocks and foot-deep holes. Tennis shoes had replaced moccasins and rubbers as our footgear for the next seventy miles. Trackers couldn't stop to retrieve rubbers sucked off in the clay. We stumbled, sprawled, picked ourselves up and struggled on.

The marsh ended abruptly at the base of high clay banks that rose sheer from the water's edge, but the change brought little improvement in footing. Instead of wallowing we were now forced to become side-hill dodgers on a steep cliff covered with loose stones. At every step our feet rolled out from under us as though we were walking on marbles. Fifty feet above us the banks leveled to support a growth of spruce and poplar. At intervals heaps of rubble and debris lay directly in our path. Landslides had brought down great masses of crumbling clay, rocks and a tangled mat of windfalls. There was no possible way of getting around these obstacles. It was just up and over, all hands joining to keep the rope free of entanglements.

Several times we forded clear-water streams that we felt sure must be teeming with brook trout. Inviting as they were, we had to pass them up. There was no time to stop and fish. Even so, evening found us camped several miles short of the goal we had set.

A day that had been packed full of adventure left the crew too keyed up to show signs of weariness. Tracking was something new and different, one more accomplishment added to their knowledge of the skills of canoemanship. They had actually enjoyed the novelty. Snarkey, who was not too husky and for whom tracking was difficult, had a viewpoint that expressed the feelings of all.

"I'm so relieved to be on dry land that tracking's a privilege, not a punishment!"

The Nelson stretched out endlessly before us as we started off on the second day. Its waters, sullied and yellow from the silt carried all the way from the prairie provinces, raced seaward between high clay banks, swirling around islands and past successions of wooded points. As we worked our way upstream away from the barren coast of Hudson Bay, the trees became larger and there were signs of increasing wildlife. Great numbers of bank swallows swooped and maneuvered, catching insects on the wing. A large osprey circled not far above the water, searching for his fish dinner. He caught sight of us, wheeled and rose to settle on the very top of a dead tree.

Whether we progressed upstream by ropes or by paddle was dictated by terrain and water levels. Several times during the second day we came to a series of points that jutted out into the river. The main force of the current was out beyond these points of land. Close to shore there were eddies that actually flowed uphill. By hugging the shore and playing the eddies, it was possible to paddle.

Unfortunately the points were often only a few hundred yards apart. Just as we seemed to be making good progress in an eddy, we would find ourselves out at the tip of a point. Wham! Before we could get around the corner, the current would hit with such fury that we either stood still or were carried backward. Then it was a matter of getting up enough steam for another try. An hour of such an ordeal made the resumption of tracking a pleasure.

The real test of manpower versus water power came on the straightaways where there were no points and no eddies. Here the banks, almost straight up and down, dropped into swift water several feet deep. With no footing whatsoever, tracking was impossible. Such stretches called for hauling in the ropes, jumping into the canoes and leaning on the paddles. Progress was made only by brute force an inch at a time. As soon as the shore line afforded footing, the track lines were once again put to use and aching arms given a rest.

Once past the junction of the Weir River, an endless vista of high steep banks on the right side made it obvious that we would have to cross to the opposite shore to find a campsite. The Nelson had narrowed to about a half-mile in width. The current was on a rampage. With bows angled upstream we put on as much steam as we could muster at the end of the day. Exhausted, we ended up a good distance below the point we had aimed for.

A strip of sand looks inviting, but it leaves much to be desired as a camping spot. With even a slight breeze it sifts and blows into everything; and it makes a very hard, unyielding bed. But we would not fuss about trifling discomforts. There might be worse ones tomorrow. Besides, it is always pleasant to fall asleep to the sound of waves lapping on the shore close to your head and a stream singing to one side of you.

For three days we tracked, while the thermometer climbed up into the eighties. There wasn't a hint of a breeze. The shore was wet and slippery and the banks were often so steep that footing disappeared. We crossed and recrossed the river.

As we neared what is designated on the map as Head of Navigation, the river increased to a mile in width. Above this point it is the shallows, reefs and rapids which make the Nelson nonnavigable for everything except canoes.

"But *we* have canoes!" sang Snarkey; then he shook his head dolefully. "More's the pity! We *have* canoes!"

There was a definite change in the shore line here. The clay banks gradually receded into the background and were replaced by benchland fifteen to twenty feet high and flat on top. The benchland was covered with loose rock, huge boulders and a growth of shrubs. The going was rough. It kept extra men busy on each tracking line holding the rope high to clear the brush and throwing it up and over points of rock so that the tracker could keep up a steady pace and maintain his forward momentum. Pulling against the full sweep of the current at the same time that he climbed over rocks and through the brush, that pace slackened, at times, to a crawl. Under the merciless sun we were drenched with perspiration and gasping for breath. But we were grateful for fair weather. Rain would have made the struggle doubly hard.

In ten hours we walked eighteen miles. In three days we had covered forty-five miles, pulling ourselves and our gear up from sea level to the hundred-foot elevation at Police Creek. To reach the railroad we were faced with climbing another eighty feet in the next twenty-five miles. Limestone Rapids of the Nelson River—miles of white water with an over-all drop of seventy-four feet—was ahead and rolling downhill to meet us.

It was humid and hot as we started the fourth day, walking along the top of the benchland. There was no footing at the base. From this high vantage point there appeared to be a flattening shore line in the distance. This was heartening for the trackers. On level ground at river level the pulling should be easy. But we had no sooner started down off the benchland than there were shouts from the bowmen. Reefs ahead!

Frantically they worked to let out the ropes and at the same time to nose out sharply away from shore. Our helmsmen were no longer enjoying a leisurely ride. With the current swirling in all directions they were feverishly letting out line, hauling it in, searching among the reefs and bars for channels deep enough and wide enough to float the canoes. Now and then their only recourse was to jump out and wade to ease the canoe over a shallows of solid limestone or one of those bars of shifting sharp pebbles and rocks. Grappling alone with a heavy craft being tossed about in the current took every ounce of strength a man had.

There was some fast and fancy footwork on the part of the trackers when it developed that the reefs extended so far out that the three-hundred-foot line was not long enough. To give the canoe room to get around the troublesome spots, the men on the ropes had to wade out into the wicked current and keep moving. Once out of the reefs, the men in harness met the full force of that current and dug in at every step, sometimes bent over almost double, struggling to make a yard at a time.

Four hours of this put five miles of the Nelson behind us. The thermometer registered 86° in the shade. Thirteen hundred air miles north of Chicago! To add to the fun, perspiring human skin attracted swarms of bulldogs—those vicious flies the size of bees that sink their stingers and hang on.

That afternoon, inching along under a sweltering sun, we came to banks of solid ice piled up to heights of ten and twelve feet.

Mike moaned, "I'm having hallucinations!"

"No, you're not," said Ben, and told us the reason for this phenomenon. Each spring during break-up, tremendous ice jams occur at the junction of the Limestone and the Nelson rivers. Carried downstream in flood stage, the ice piles up along the shore to forty-foot heights, gouging into the base of the steep clay banks. According to the Indians, it is a horrifying sight. Tracking up this portion of the Nelson earlier in the season is extremely dangerous. As the river recedes from flood stage it leaves grottoes with a ceiling of ice over the heads of the trackers. Later on, as they thaw, these walls give way suddenly, bringing with them debris and boulders to crush anything that might be in their path.

Now on July 31st the remains, though not dangerous, were still impressive. All day Ben had been taking advantage of perfect lighting to get a picture story of our experiences. When he aimed the camera for a movie of Snarkey picking his way along a narrow strip of gravel and broken limestone between the wall of ice and the rushing river, pulling on the tracking line like a workhorse, one of the other boys declared, "He gets in a movie because he thinks tracking's a privilege." But Snarkey's expression said something else. He was obviously wondering why he had ever left home.

Within sight of Lower Limestone Rapids we were stopped dead in our tracks by cliffs rising to two hundred feet and dropping precipitously into a deep, fast channel. The river had to be crossed. The ropes were hauled in and we struggled across to a large island near the left bank. This was the foot of the rapids. White water, miles of it, rolled downhill to meet us. Tracking lines would snap against it. It was utterly impossible to paddle. Steep banks with no footing at the base made lining or portaging hopeless.

"What do we do now?"

"We wade," said the Chief. "Four to a canoe, shore side. Watch the bows; keep 'em in!"

So we waded the rapids, inch by inch, stepping into holes, fighting to stand against the force of the current. Once Orie sprawled in the horizontal, clutching at the gunwales. For seconds he just hung on, while the rest of his crew struggled to tow him as well as the canoe until he could get himself upended. It was three hours before we made camp, not quite three miles up the rapids.

Near the campsite the world showed a confusing conglomeration of seasons. Sandpiper babies with the shells still clinging to them, and a long way to go this fall; they would have to grow astoundingly fast to develop wings strong enough to carry them. Asters and goldenrod were up; yet spring flowers were still in bloom. In the Far North, where the time between snowfalls is so short, nature is hard put to produce four seasons. She seems to solve the problem by squeezing spring, summer and fall so close together that they get all mixed up.

12

Paddles Rest

NOW THAT THE WORST OF LIMESTONE RAPIDS WAS behind us, only a few more miles separated us from the railroad. We had been moving so slowly for the past few days that when we broke camp in the morning we could almost see our evening's destination. This was the case as we headed for the tracks, and the day was going to be another tough one.

The rest of this stretch of white water was too deep to wade. Tracking was our only choice, even though this shaded left bank was wet and hazardous. Until we were beyond the rapids it would be impossible to cross to the sun-dried side. The men in harness started off bravely through waist-high grass along the marshy shore—and before they had taken the slack out of the ropes they were wallowing in mud. As soon as the canoes were loose in the current, the tracking lines tightened with a zing and jerked the trackers to a standstill.

All hands grabbed the ropes. Step by step, sinking sometimes to our knees in that mud, we tugged the canoes along and prayed that the ropes would hold. Out in the rapids the rest of the crew were praying even harder.

Somebody remarked that we had not had dry feet since leaving York Factory, and that made all of us dwell on our foot troubles! Hiking ten or fifteen miles a day in tennis shoes over sharp rocks and gravel had left us suffering from stone bruises. Grinding sand had taken the skin off our toes. We longed for the railroad tracks. We would do nothing but sit for three days and more.

"Heaven, that's what it'll be," murmured Snarkey. "Pure heaven."

More white water, more tracking—once on a broad rock shelf that was a tracker's paradise, if he had to walk at all—and finally a short paddle, and we came into a bay that marked the portage to the railroad. For the time being we were parting company with the Nelson. From here it courses far to the westward through a series of wicked gorges, falls and rapids. To return to Norway House by continuing on this meandering loop would require several extra weeks of arduous canoe travel. The Churchill railroad made it possible for us to cut off the loop.

This was one point on our summer's schedule where we had to be on time. The train ran only once a week. Being even a few hours late would have left us stranded. We were not only on time, we were three days ahead of schedule. Orie and John could now catch the northbound train and have a day around the Churchill settlement to pursue their botanical studies.

As the three canoes nosed into the clay bank at the portage landing, the weary crew mustered enough energy for triumphal shouts.

"Save it," said Ben. "Our day's work isn't over. We've got a man-killer of a portage to make yet."

The railroad tracks were a good two hundred and fifty feet above the river bank where we stood unloading our gear. And that two hundred and fifty feet was so nearly straight up it would have been a challenge to an army mule. By digging in sidewise over a zigzag course, one slow step at a time, burdened under the tumpline loads, winding up and up, redfaced, dripping with perspiration and gasping for breath, we made it. Then down again for another load. And a final quarter-mile push through the brush to our trackside camp at what is known as Mile 352. What else can you name a flag stop in the middle of nowhere?

"May I never go through anything like this day again," prayed Fred fervently. "As long as I live!"

Snarkey, pleased with an earlier comment he had dreamed up, explained to the rest of us, "He's highstrung enough as it is. The nervous type."

At nine-thirty next morning we heard the rumble

of the approaching northbound train. Everybody
gathered to flag her down, and Orie and John
boarded it to catch a glimpse of the Barren Lands
beyond the limit of trees.

The rest of us stayed in camp to tackle the unpleas-
ant but necessary task of getting ourselves and our
equipment thoroughly washed and aired in prepara-
tion for boarding a train. Some of the boys had not
washed their clothes all summer. The drenching
rains and days of wading, they reasoned, had taken
care of all their laundry needs.

"That's what you think!" said Ben. "On the
double, guys! There's a stream underneath the trestle
about half a mile up the road."

We even scrubbed the canoes with Ivory soap.

Our arrival at Mile 352 had ostensibly brought
us out of the isolation of the wilderness to a direct
link with civilization. It could hardly be said that the
roar of traffic was annoying. Nor was our privacy in-
vaded in the least. During our entire three-day encampment, just one northbound work train passed
by with a load of gravel and a crew for repairing the
roadbed.

"Must wear out from disuse," said Chuck and
Franklin as they sat sunning two bad cases of foot
rash and vowing never to wear wet, dirty wool socks
again. "Is there ever much traffic on this railroad,
Chief?"

"It carries grain to the elevators at Churchill for
shipment to England," said Ben. "But that's not the

only reason its maintenance is mighty important. It's the only means of modern ground transportation through hundreds of thousands of square miles. Maintenance could be vital from a military standpoint—in case!"

The weekly southbound "Muskeg Special" was supposed to be due at two-thirty in the afternoon of the third day. We were taking no chances. By noon our canoes, boxes and packs were lined up along the tracks and each of us was posted as to which pieces of freight he was responsible for getting aboard. Then Ben asked what he thought was merely a rhetorical question. "Everybody had a bath?"

There was a sudden silence.

"Well?"

"No," said Franklin and Chuck half-heartedly.

"No," said Fred.

Ben threw his hands in the air. "I thought I said it was an order when we first got here! Do you want the other train passengers sniffing and taking seats at the other end of the car? You won't be in the fresh air. Get down to that stream on the double!"

Grinning, the three of them loped off. "And run all the way back!" Ben shouted after them.

At two-fifteen they were still missing. They were not even in sight. At one minute to train time Franklin and Chuck came on the run.

"Fred's wallet dropped into the water and he's still hunting for it!"

"Wallets, wallets!" stormed Ben.

We all remembered what had happened on Hudson Bay only too well. This time we would have been stranded for a week at Mile 352 if the train had not been two hours late.

The "Special" was a string of freights with an immigration car tacked on the rear for the accommodation of stray passengers. There were John and Orie waiting for us, four tourists playing cards, and the "newsy" who was also the cook. We devoured the jellied canned meat and fried potatoes he offered us. Except for bacon, fish and one treasured can of ham, we had not tasted a piece of meat for weeks, nor seen a potato since starting down the God's River.

For the first time in six weeks the Ferrier party was moving without exerting a muscle. About all that could be said for the change from paddle propulsion to steam locomotion was that it was easier. The change in speed was not as startling as we had expected. The scenery was not whizzing by at anything resembling a dizzy rate. The "Muskeg Special" was in no hurry. Rolling lazily over a roadbed laid along monotonously flat ridges of scrubby timber, she slowed to a crawl to cross a thousand-foot steel span high above Kettle Rapids, a spectacular gorge of the Nelson.

This was the first rapids we had seen all summer

that we could gaze at without wondering what we were going to do about it. We looked down into the boiling cauldron and realized that we were actually being carried past it. We were not a part of it. And its splendor somehow had no more meaning than if we had viewed it on a picture postcard.

"You know," said Art, "I've done a lot of traveling, and I can't help feeling sorry for the tourists who get their impressions of this country by excursion train. You can't really see lakes and rivers or get to know the North, or anywhere else, through a train window."

There was no such thing as a change of crews on the "Muskeg Special." One outfit took her all the way up from Winnipeg and back. When their eight-hour working day was over, the train sat where it was and waited until the crew was ready to go back on duty the following day. The extended stop was at the village of Gillam; Hudson's Bay Company, railroad shops, mission, trappers' homes. The evening was ours to take in the town.

We had been without mail all summer, and we had looked forward to the possibility that here, at last, there might be word from home waiting for us. But all mail for the Ferrier party had left Gillam two days before we arrived; it was bound for York Factory! Via canoe!

Snarkey rumpled his red hair in mock fury. "I told my folks when I left Illinois," he remarked, "that they needn't bother to write, because the only way I

could get a letter would be to hire an Indian runner
to try to find me. And they didn't believe it!"

When the manager of the Hudson's Bay Company
post offered to take off our hands any food that we
might be carrying in excess of our needs, we used the
trading post as a trading post indeed. Here in the
wilderness, exchange and barter is the rule of the
day. We gave the manager pudding powders and dehydrated vegetables, and tasted the first fresh fruit
we had had in many weeks.

Late in the evening we groped our way back to the
"Muskeg Special" and stretched out on the seats. The
poker game was still going on, this time with the railroad men included. It was hard to sleep; the car was
stuffy as well as noisy and we were used to the out-of-
doors. Then three of us got sick, and we all were made
aware once more of the fact that wilderness survival
depends on caution and common sense. At Mile 352
the stream had looked a bit muddy, but we had not
taken the simple precaution of boiling our drinking
water.

"Funny," murmured Steve sleepily across the
seats, "you'd think being propelled without any exertion would be a real treat. It isn't. Anybody agree?"

Several voices agreed. "Treat?" said Chuck. "It's an
ordeal."

In twenty-two hours on that train we traveled one
hundred and sixty-six miles, an average of seven
miles an hour! Even so, the rate at which we moved
south brought a noticeably more rapid transition in

topography, climatic conditions and plant growth than we had experienced in our northward trek. Instead of gradual change, the difference in just one day was striking. Balsam fir, sparse or nonexistent farther north, was now common. The timber in general increased in girth and height. All the flowers along the tracks were typical of late summer and early fall.

August 5th brought Mile 186, the village of Thicket Portage, on the main canoe route from the Nelson River to the Churchill River by way of Nelson House. This was the place for us to pick up our paddles again.

For centuries before the coming of the railroad, the village had been part of a well-traveled highway, the water highway of the fur trade. After the Canadian National Railroad came through, Thicket Portage became a crossroads and developed into one of the largest settlements in the five hundred miles between the Pas and Churchill. There were *two* stores in town, and even a small hotel.

It was at Thicket Portage that we had a chance to examine at close range an elusive animal we had only glimpsed along the trail—in spite of all the water we had followed. The game guardian, counterpart of the United States wardens, took us into the bush to show us twenty live beavers. They had been caught, unharmed, and were temporarily confined in cages, ready to be redistributed around the country and released to establish new houses.

More often than we had seen them in the wilderness, we had heard the resounding slap of flat tail on water, their warning signal of our approach. Rounding a bend, we would come upon the evidence that a crew of construction engineers had been hard at work —a lodge, a dam, freshly felled poplars, and stumps covered with incisor marks. But the engineers did not choose to work under the surveillance of human eyes.

In our conversation with the warden it evolved that education is the keynote in game management. The Indian of the Far North, with his philosophy of living for today, has been accused of wasteful slaughter and of being the cause of decreasing game population. But white men are often just as greedy and just as guilty. They must be made to realize that laws are made for their protection to prevent the depletion of the supply of animals upon which they depend for fur and for food.

The regulations relating to beaver are just an example. There must be at least seven live beaver houses on a trapper's line. If there are seven or more houses, he may take just one beaver from each house yearly. One of the game guardian's many duties is to make an inspection tour to count the number of houses on each trap line. The number of skins a trapper turns in for sale cannot exceed the number of houses on the check list.

Probably even more important than laws and regulations is the enlistment of the co-operation of every trapper. The Canadian government has a program to teach him how to improve his territory and provide the best possible habitat. If it can be demonstrated to him that by insuring suitable food and cover, building small dams to maintain water levels, and taking the trouble to control predatory enemies, he can increase his yield, the whole thing makes sense. The more he produces, the bigger his harvest.

Our bout with civilization this time ended in an incident which the crew turned into a horrible practical joke. They had spent the evening in the village. The natives had made ice cream for them and had sent some to Ben and me as a special treat. By flashlight we dug some spoons out of the chuck box and drove in. The first taste told us there was definitely a queer flavor. I tried bravely to swallow another mouthful to show my appreciation to them for lugging it all the way across the portage. It had been very thoughtful. But the stuff was so horrible I was almost gagging. Just as I tried to take one more bite, someone flashed a light and revealed the awful face I was making. The camp broke into guffaws. The ice cream had been mixed in a discarded gasoline drum.

13

The Fish Are Jumping

THIS WAS THE LAST LAP—THE HOME STRETCH. IN A way we had saved the best until the last. Portaging, which had been a grueling endurance contest and a punishment early in the summer, was now easy. That ton of food we started with had been whittled down to a few boxes and waterproof bags; and we were hardened to take almost anything. Flies and mosquitoes, which had made life almost intolerable in June and July had now, in August, nearly disappeared. Scenically this was probably the most beautiful part of the whole thousand miles. With the crossing of Thicket Portage we left behind the sand, clay and gravel area to re-enter the rugged granite rock country.

From here on we were assured of beautifully timbered points or islands for campsites with tents pitched on a springy carpet of duff; clean flat rocks for cooking; no more sand in food or dunnage; good fishing waters. A week of stiff upstream travel, bucking the powerful current of the Nelson River, might prove too strenuous for neophytes, but not for us. The botanists, after many weeks of tough work under difficult circumstances, could now relax to some extent. They would continue to search for and collect new specimens to complete their job, but the data from this well-traveled accessible area was not as vital or important as that procured from the back of beyond.

We nosed away from the portage and headed off down Landing Lake. After a four-day respite it felt good to be swinging the paddles. The lake was long, narrow, heavily-timbered, its shore line broken by lovely points and wooded islands, the smallest mere rockpiles sentineled by a lone spruce, the largest perhaps three acres. With its beauty and endless waterways into superb fishing country, this was what any outdoor enthusiast and nature lover would call paradise.

We were moving much too slowly. Relaxation should not mean dying on the job. But our contacts with any sign of civilization, no matter how few or far between, always seemed to upset the smooth running of the expedition. It is always a relief to shove away from the settlements. They are an intrusion on the tranquility that comes with complete isolation from the outside world. After even brief breaks in our routine of trail life, it takes a few days of adjustment to get back into harness. Digestive tracts are out of kilter from munching on snacks between meals. The energy required for a ten- or twelve-hour day of hard work is noticeably lacking. In trail language this crew was afflicted with "Chinese rheumatism," a disease caused by iron in the blood turning to lead in the tail.

"What's the trouble, guys? We can't afford to dawdle." That was Ben at lunch time.

There were grins, but little spirit of rallying. Somebody offered an old excuse. "We're saving our energy."

"For what?"

"Oh—for Cross Portage. Didn't you say that was where we get back into the Nelson?"

"That's right."

"And it's two miles long?"

Ben nodded. Several crew members groaned.

"Yeah, I think we need to have plenty of energy when we hit that."

They were in no hurry to get there. But under prodding they made it down Landing Lake, into a weedy bay, up a small creek; and then the misery could be put off no longer.

As portages go, there is nothing difficult about Cross Portage except its length, and our supplies by now were so cut down in weight and bulk that we could complete the job in two trips. For centuries this portage had been on one of the main arteries of the fur trade. The great York boats had used this route on their way to and from Nelson House, seventy-five miles to the northwest. At the present time it is still one of the most heavily-traveled canoe trails; in recent years, with the coming of the railroad, the portage has become very busy. The Nelson River is open to commercial fishermen. Using hundred-foot nets of six-inch mesh, they bring in sturgeon weighing up to a hundred pounds apiece. The catch runs into tons, and is hauled by horse and wagon over Cross Portage on the way to "the steel" for shipment. All this traffic makes not only a well-beaten path but a road. To reach the other end all we had to do was plunk one foot in front of the other; no struggle at all; yet the crew fairly dragged through the woods.

And when we shoved off from Cross Portage camp on the morning of August 7th, they were still dragging.

Mother Nature gave us a hand and helped to make up for what we lacked in push by sending us off with a brisk tailwind. Directly ahead of us the Nelson spread out all over the map to become Sipewesk Lake. This so-called lake, which is about fifteen miles wide and forty miles long, had countless deep bays, arms leading into blind alleys, and hundreds of islands around which the current of the Nelson swishes in every direction.

Supposedly there are three main channels. But it takes a wizard of a navigator to find a channel and stay with it. In such a labyrinth one wrong turn might find us hours later at a dead end. Our schedule was too tight to allow for bewilderment and wandering around Sipewesk. The map was inaccurate and entirely undependable. By sticking to a general southwesterly course and keeping eyes peeled for signs of campfires and Indian guideposts to assure us from time to time that we were on the right road, we managed somehow to keep to course.

The steadily blowing tailwind gave the boys an idea. "Hey, Chief, how's about putting up sails? You know Crees never paddle when they can get Mother Nature to do the work."

Ben shook his head. More Chinese rheumatism. Sailing is supposed to be a lazy man's delight. It may be if you are cruising along with an empty canoe.

We had already tried sailing à la Cree. Our experiences had left us with the opinion that, with a loaded canoe, it usually saves neither time nor effort. At least for a white man. It usually worked like this:

First you go ashore and cut spruce poles suitable in length and size for a mast and a boom. The boom is tied about midway up the mast and forks up at an angle. To the poles is fastened a blanket, poncho, or anything you happen to have. The skipper's controls consist of ropes or the thongs of a tumpline tied top and bottom to one side of the square sail. The contraption is now ready to be hoisted upright in the bow.

Meanwhile, to keep ballast low, all the dunnage has to be rearranged to clear out holes so that passengers can sit in the bottom of the canoe. The procedure thus far has kept you struggling for an hour or more.

Ready to embark, you find that the rigging cuts off all view of what lies ahead. So one man squeezes himself in the pointed bow to watch for rocks. But he can't just sit and enjoy his cramped quarters. If the wind is anything stronger than a slight breeze, he has to contort himself in position to brace the wobbly mast. The helmsman, ruddering from the stern, has to be prepared for almost anything. With the sail in his way, he steers blind, depending on his bowman for directions. His watchman yells something or other, but with a tailwind his voice doesn't carry backward. The shouting back and forth becomes a bedlam. Meanwhile the middleman is getting it in the neck from everyone. If you are going too slow or too fast, it's all his fault for the way he is handling the sail.

Like as not, just as you get moving along nicely, the boom starts slipping. Or a good strong gust of wind comes along. Crack! There goes the main mast! If the wind is too strong, you move so fast that the waves start sloshing over the side. If it isn't strong enough you go at a snail's pace. Then it dies altogether. You are becalmed. So you go ashore and waste another hour dismantling the outfit and re-arranging duffel so you can start paddling again.

On Sipewesk we were not yet in a clear-cut channel. It was deep in spots, but there were shallows to be watched for. Sand bars formed from Nelson River silt came very close to the surface. Rollers surging ahead of the brisk breeze were too high to risk using the Cree sail. But the boys kept on begging, and finally the Chief compromised. The middlemen could sit in the bottom and stretch a poncho between them. By bracing the top corners with paddles, they would have an improvised sail that would catch as much wind as we could take with safety.

The ponchos billowed and snapped. The waves kept getting higher and higher to make the stern man's job no picnic. Ruddering to hit them at just the right angle took both strength and concentration. The rollers were long, even and undulating. We were riding them like corks, and the other canoes disappeared in the troughs. Even though this was upstream travel against the current, the thirty-mile-an-hour tailwind, caught in our improvised sails, pushed us along at a fair speed. At least it gave the crew a few more hours to snap out of their lethargy.

Ben said, "I feel a jacking-up lecture coming on."

What brought the lecture to a head, however, was his discovery that the crew had worked out a plan to use up food and therefore have less to portage—they were so sure we had more than enough for the short time left on the trail. They were cooking up twice as much as we could possibly eat, and great panfuls were being thrown away every day.

Once more his language was not for polite society. When he calmed down, he declared, "All right, I'm a spoil-sport. I'm too cautious! I'm an old meanie! But in twenty-five years and thirty-five thousand canoe miles I have never had a wild adventure or a serious accident. And that record is going to stand! How would you like bad weather to hold us up so long that we couldn't make Norway House in time for the boat? How would we feed twelve people for an extra week without any groceries? Tell me, how? I ask you!"

Everybody was looking sheepish by that time, and Ben softened his voice another few notches. "I guess you hadn't thought of that when you got your bright idea, eh? For wilderness survival, you've got to think all the time. I'll quote Stefansson again: 'If everything is well-managed, if there are no miscalculations or mistakes, then the things that happen are only the things you expected to happen and with which you can therefore deal.' I agree with Stefansson.

"If everything goes well we have ample time to reach Norway House on schedule. But you can't travel a hundred and eighty miles upstream in one week at the rate you have been going since we left Thicket Portage. This morning you sailed. From here on in, we paddle."

During the afternoon the horsepower picked up!

Sipewesk is an Indian word meaning "water of many islands." The name is appropriate. There are hundreds of islands; but for the white man to say "lake" is somewhat farfetched. It was anything but a standing body of water. That lake was moving—and fast. The techniques of canoemanship were definitely those of river travel. Whenever possible, to escape the sweeping current, we hugged the shore line and played the eddies. Then, meeting a riffles head on, progress would be slowed almost to a standstill. That called for putting on extra steam.

At the Narrows of Sipewesk the Nelson River collects itself for a short stretch to flow through a well-defined channel. Beyond the Narrows it spreads again to become a lake that is very wide and open. Up to this point islands had provided protection from the wind. The open stretch was wild. One look, as we emerged from the Narrows, was enough to convince us that an attempt to cross would be foolhardy. Whether we liked it or not, we were forced to stop several miles short of the goal we had set for the day.

In a howling wind we headed for the lee side of the nearest island. Regardless of what kind of campsite it might provide, this was where we would have to stay until the lake calmed down. Luck was with us. The site was not only suitable, it was a gem. Made to order and sitting there waiting for us, a gently-sloping point of clean granite jutted out to form not only a snug calm harbor but also an ideal spot for a campfire, with plenty of space for twelve people to spread out.

Sleeping quarters were in a lush forest. Moss, inches deep, completely covered the ground, the rocks, and the windfalls. On this springy velvet mattress, tents were pitched. It seemed a sacrilege to trample on it. Moss is slow-growing. The mattress had been many years in the making. "Wish there were someplace else to step," said Ben.

There were chuckles from the crew, and John said,

"If you *will* come out here, Chief, even you can't avoid leaving a man-made scar behind you!"

The rising call came at five o'clock. We were going to take advantage of the fact that a wind often abates somewhat in the early morning, and then whips up again later in the day. The sky was gray and the air chilly, and the waves were still rolling a bit too high for comfort, but the Chief's decision was that we could make the crossing safely.

At the end of the lake the waters of the Nelson converged once again, narrowing into a channel that flowed between high granite shores. This section of the river, one of several channels, was the most direct route from Sipewesk to Cross Lake.

Sipewesk has an elevation of 598 feet. Cross Lake is 679 feet above sea level. Between the two, a distance of about 40 miles, the Nelson was flowing downhill and dropping 81 feet over riffles, rapids and falls to meet us.

Noon found us portaging at Chain-of-Rock Rapids, and on the off chance that there might just happen to be a fish sporting around in the white water, Mike dug out his rod and reel while the cooks were getting lunch. On the third cast the rod bent, the reel started spinning. Mike braced himself and the battle was on. When he brought in a twenty-five-pound, forty-two-inch northern pike, the expression on his face sent Ben running for the camera.

"Great Jumping Northern Pike! Look what the Runt caught!" shouted Snarkey, and ran for his own rod and reel. Steve was already casting. Where that one came from, there should be more. They were ready to forego lunch if necessary. Steve and Mike would rather fish than eat, anyway.

In a matter of minutes that rapids was full of lines, and the fish were jumping for the fun of it. Or to get out of each other's way. They grabbed anything that was thrown at them. Mike's, though, was the grand-daddy and all we could use for food, so the rest were thrown back to leap another day.

As we neared Red Rock we could see the Nelson dropping into our laps over a series of rapids and three small falls. For the rest of the afternoon there wasn't a dull moment. These rapids called for lining, and once again we were hearing the old refrain, "Keep those canoes off the rocks. Don't let those canoes bang on shore." Two men out of every three dropped to their haunches and started hopping along like jack rabbits, using paddles and now and then an outflung foot as bumpers, while the human draft horse on the fifty-foot rope pulled against the powerful sweep of the river.

Each of the three falls required unloading, carry-ing, reloading. A precarious landing at the foot of the first falls—a portage of a few rods over a steep hill, steep going up and steep coming down the other side —then put in and paddle seventy-five yards. A second falls. Unload, lift up over a rock ledge. Reload. Paddle another two hundred yards. A third falls—unload— portage fifty yards.

Camp at last. With no insects! There were things to be grateful for in this world.

In June and July we had seldom seen darkness, but now the days were noticeably shorter. We noted many such changes of season, and we began to realize that the everyday, run-of-the-mill scenery was on the spectacular side. Earth and sky and water were putting on a breathtaking show.

At Hill Rapids the Nelson cascades over a ten-foot drop. The portage, up and over the hill for which it is named, was treacherously steep and very slippery. On a well-traveled route such as this, the portages are kept cut out and cleared; there are no windfalls. But there is never any way of making a straight up-and-down hill less so. That portage was a killer, especially for the men with their heads inside the canoes! Slipping, slithering, almost sprawling; catching themselves; steady; then slip and slither along again. And it was worse going down.

Once more afloat beyond the hill, we resorted to every trick we knew to outsmart the current in approaching the next rapids. For miles below them and for an hour or more before they came into view, we were reading the announcement cards. Strings of foamy bubbles came dancing and bobbing toward us as the current swept, arced, and swung crazily. Saucer-shaped whirlpools of all sizes swirled and sucked ominously. A sound that at first resembled a sighing wind in the treetops became a muffled swishing that gradually increased in volume. Rounding a bend we saw the cause of all the noise. We were hemmed in between walls of solid granite. Above the rapids all channels of the Nelson converged.

The entire river with its tremendous volume of water was squeezed together and pouring over a gradual drop. As we came closer the crescendo of sound became a thunderous roar, and the approach to the portage landing was frightening and difficult.

"Chief! Chief! How do we manage this?"

"Hug the cliff!"

Alongside the cliff wall and with fierce, frantic strokes we inched forward to a point where the shore lines fanned out and flattened. This was Bladder Rapids. It stretched as far as the eye could see.

Safely on shore and unloaded, we took time to stand and look with awe at the surging power. Any attempts at questions or comments would have been useless. Human voices could not have been heard.

The portage around the Bladder's rim, a wide, spongy, moss-covered trail through lush forest, was no punishment. Above the rapids we put in and paddled on up the channel which led to Whitemud Falls. The river here was flowing through a fault in the granite said to be over a hundred feet deep. That gave us some idea of the amount of water carried by the Nelson.

Paddles swung rhythmically and steadily. We wanted to reach Whitemud Falls, our third and last portage of the day, and pitch camp early. Whitemud was too spectacular to give it just a passing glance.

The sooner we reached camp the more time we would have to walk to the falls, some distance off the trail, and enjoy what was the highlight of the whole summer when it came to scenic beauty.

The portage trail, well over a half-mile in length, ends in a dismal swamp. The plan was that six members of the crew would carry the three canoes over on their first trip, wade through the swamp, float them as soon as they reached open water, and paddle around a corner to the high rock point that afforded a campsite. The rest of us, starting off with tumpline loads, were to follow, but veer off the trail to the left and meet them in camp. Just where we were to veer or how far to the left was anybody's guess. The portage trail was so wide that we could have marched four abreast, but we found not even a hint of any branching path that might take us to camp. Six people had six different ideas of how to get where we were going. Six different people were determined to lead the way. In the dense forest it was only a matter of minutes before each of us, launching off on his own, completely lost sight of his comrades.

Much later—it took us more than an hour to find our way through the forest and into camp—Ben learned what we had done, and he gave us a dressing-down we didn't forget. "You could have been lost for days!"

"Ah, Chief, we weren't lost; we were only—uh—temporarily bewildered."

"You were lost and you know it. And I'm ashamed

of you because you were long ago told one of the first rules of woodsmanship: in the wilderness, stick together. *Stick together.* Your survival may depend on it."

We weren't ready to admit it out loud, but each of us six smart-alecks knew the Chief was right. It had been mighty bewildering alone in the forest, and I for one had felt more than a little panicky before I had found the daylight again.

14

Whitemud

THE FOLLOWING DAY SYMPTOMS OF THAT OLD RHEU-
matism were acute. The woodchoppers were so late in
crawling out of their sacks, and so slow in gathering
wood, that we began to wonder if breakfast would
ever be ready. The dishwashers were barely able to
lift one dish at a time. There were murmurings like
"What's the difference? What's the rush? You can almost smell Norway House now."

"I'll tell you," the Chief cut into the murmurs.
"This is the tenth of August. The *Keenora* is due on
the fourteenth. We should be at Norway House or its
immediate vicinity by the evening of the twelfth. We
need a full free day. You want to be fit to mingle with
the boat passengers, don't you? Then you've got to
have time to clean up yourself and your possessions.
And things have to go to the Company to be stored

till next summer. You may not be coming with me next summer, but you've used the gear this time, and by golly, you're partly responsible for it."

Then he smiled. "Gee whiz, as Mike says—don't make me do it all. I'm getting on in years!"

The Chief could make them angry but he could always get them back on his side again.

"Come on, there, gang, step on it!" That was Chuck. "All those over twenty as well as those under! When the weather's good, we travel. We might not get to another day."

And everybody stepped on it.

Regardless of the tight schedule, we took two hours to visit Whitemud Falls. The sight was one we could not pass up. A canoeman has great respect for Whitemud. He gives her a wide berth. To avoid committing suicide, in approaching from either above or below he does not paddle within sight of the falls. To see them requires taking the time and effort to walk quite some distance off to one side of the portage trail.

Though many feet pass over the portage on this route, the path to the falls was so faint as to be difficult to follow, and indicated that they were rarely visited. Consequently their beauty was entirely unspoiled. With very little imagination we could pretend that we had discovered this marvel of nature, for there was not a sign of anyone ever having been there.

Above the falls about two-thirds of the Nelson

River pours swiftly, but with a deceptively smooth, syrupy appearance, through one channel that narrows to around two hundred yards. At the brink this tremendous mass finds its way through clefts in the solid granite and emerges as three separate falls. With a thunderous roar the waters drop thirty feet into a gorge cut between rock walls that rise to heights of two hundred feet.

As the falls strike the rocks below, mountains of foam and spray are tossed thirty feet in the air. Can this be the murky yellow silt-laden Nelson? In the seething cauldron the mud has been churned to a dazzling white. Whitemud. And more water pouring over it in twenty-four hours, they say, than flows over Niagara in a week.

The effect of the sight upon our crew approached hypnosis. They stared, and moved closer. Closer still. They did not seem to see the Chief's violent gestures.

"Get back! Get back!" He shouted, and his voice was a whisper.

Art and Walt, John and Orie, and all the boys moved on toward the falls. They had to have a better view—and then a better one.

Ben raced to the two farthest in front and with outstretched arms blocked their way. "I said stay back!" This point, and no farther, he thought, was safe.

Suddenly the beauty became terrifying, as a solid wall of water moved toward us in one gigantic forty-foot wave that surged up out of the gorge and rolled over the top of the bank. As it broke, the wash came much too close for comfort, and was still straining at us as it receded. We needed no more warnings.

"Wow!" said Fred.

"That expresses it," nodded Snarkey.

A duck hawk, that pointed-winged falcon, dove past us suddenly with the speed of a bullet, too fast for our eyes to follow his flight, and then soared up and off again with his breakfast. As he disappeared, a rainbow arced across the spray of the falls.

Walking back to camp, Ben was talking to the crew about water power, dams, flood control—and nature's horse sense. Our route had taken us through a country of heavy rainfall where over half the earth's surface is covered by water. Yet floods are unknown. The fluctuation in water levels is by a gradual rise and fall. Forests, marshes, bogs, lakes and ponds are the sponges and reservoirs here, and nothing else is needed. Surely this was convincing proof that flood control depends on holding back the water where it falls. What was the sense to the destruction of forests, the drainage of marshes, the tilling of fields to provide more agricultural land if all the great dams in the country could not stop the waters when they wanted to flood and ruin that very land?

"I hope I never see it here," Ben said. "The world's pretty good as created."

"I agree," said Steve.

John added, "Chief, you almost make a man feel a personal responsibility to see that what is left that way—as created, I mean—stays that way!"

Ben sighed. "Well, Canada's a big country, and a wealthy one, and it's bound to be 'developed,'—as they call it. The North is bound to change. But I hope the value of the wilderness won't be forgotten until it's too late."

Whitemud came very near the end of our eight-weeks' expedition. What we had seen along the way was typical of thousands of square miles of Canada. Our own thousand-mile circle was only a speck on the map.

Between Whitemud Falls and Cross Lake the Nelson never let us forget for one minute that we were going up and she was coming down. If we insisted on bucking her, it was up to us to find a way to match our strength against hers. To paddle every inch possible was a challenge. Whenever, in spite of fast-flying blades, we were stopped dead in our tracks, she still didn't have us licked. There were other means of making headway. Fast current and white water, hour after hour, called for such frequent changes in technique that we were jumping in and out of the canoes like grasshoppers. We paddled. We lined, with two painters tied bow and stern. We roped. When all else failed we portaged.

On one of the portages we met a party of about 24 Indians who, when they saw we were white men, proceeded to show us how the job should be done. Obviously they were exhibiting their prowess for our benefit. One behind the other in single file, men, women, and children, they came running at a dog-trot.

"Gosh," said Mike with awe, "look at those loads. It makes my knees buckle to watch 'em. And they've still got breath enough to giggle and chatter!"

There wasn't one husky-looking man in the lot. Not only were they slight of build, but so thin that they appeared to be undernourished. When one of our crew said, "Hey, look at *him!*" we concentrated our attention on a man who couldn't have tipped the scales at more than a hundred and forty. First he tied the thongs of his tumpline around two wood boxes. Each box contained sixty pounds of bacon. The way he lifted them on his back and eased the head strap in place, you might think they were packed with cotton. Over the top of the boxes went a hundred-pound sack of flour. As another hundred-pound sack was tossed on top of his head lengthwise to offset the backward pull, he gave a wiggle of the shoulders and a punch or two at the sacks to get balanced and off he went. He was toting a load of three hundred and twenty pounds. And he didn't stagger. He loped off!

A ten-year-old boy who followed him was carrying eighty pounds. That was the answer. The Indian children grow up with the tumpline. If a boy aspires to be a packer for the Hudson's Bay Company, he must, by the time he reaches maturity, be able to carry a minimum of two hundred and fifty pounds. On the canoe trails in the United States, the white man who crosses a portage with a hundred pounds considers himself quite the Goliath. Members of the Ferrier crew were no slouches when it came to portaging. We were very proud of developing neck and back muscles that would take on a load equivalent to our own weight. But those Indians were making monkeys of us.

We decided that these must be Cross Lake Crees who have the reputation of being ambitious. Like most other natives, they trap during the winter. But unlike the typical Indian, who spends the rest of the year fishing, loafing and lounging around the posts, many at the Cross Lake settlement find remunerative work for the summer months. Some travel as far as the prairies when extra hands are needed on the wheat farms at threshing time. A few get jobs along the Churchill railroad, others in the Lake Winnipeg fisheries.

As we entered Cross Lake and worked our way over its shallows and along channels sweeping around islands, we noted another evidence of the industriousness of these Indians. Along the shores rectangular enclosures, surrounded by logs, held quite sizable and flourishing vegetable gardens. In a country of bare, uneven, solid rock, a garden is "built" by slow hard work. Soil of any kind is so scarce that it must be laboriously gathered and stored so that it won't wash away.

The nearer we drew to Norway House the more often the boys mentioned home; what they were going to do when they got there; and especially what they were going to eat. "Camp food tastes pretty flat when you let yourself start dreaming of broiled steaks, lemon meringue pie and hot fudge sundaes," Franklin declared, and Snarkey agreed. "You're not kidding, Piggy."

Between Cross Lake and Norway House the Nelson wends its way by devious routes. We chose to follow the scenic eastern channel by way of Pipestone Lake. The river narrows and twists through shadowy, cool, rocky gorges. We half expected to see canoes coming toward us as we turned the corners, for the channel we followed was an arterial of traffic that was well-traveled. Well-traveled, that is, in the language of the North. This was our sixth day out of Thicket Portage. We had seen two parties in the six days: an Indian family camped on Cross Portage and those we had just met on the trail. On this main highway, congestion was no problem.

Upstream river work, though it may be tiring, is never tiresome. Our twelve-man outfit had had some stiff training, but our opponent had been at the game for countless centuries. His power was gradually diminishing now, where diverging channels split it. But we still had a battle. The Nelson would always give men battle.

Sometimes, of course, it's not the river that causes trouble; it's carelessness, as the Chief kept insisting.

I attempted a flying leap from canoe to shore, missed by about a foot, and illustrated the point! Below the water line, and dropping sheerly to depths of several feet, the rock was covered with a thick coat of slime. I clutched frantically to keep from sliding to the bottom of that greased toboggan, but I was in up to my ears before they fished me out.

"Gee, Marion, are you O.K.?" That was the boys. But the Chief just looked disgusted!

At Sugar Falls the river tumbles off a shallow rock ledge that extends across its entire width, not as one falls but as dozens of little ones of irregular heights. At a few spots the rock ledge dips, inviting you to get out and give just a hefty lift to get up and over without unloading your canoes. We spent an hour trying.

A storm was brewing, and so at last we gave up and headed for shore. The tents were pitched just in time; it was a real downpour. Undaunted, the anglers stood out in the rain and started casting from shore. It might be a long time before they had a chance like this again. Besides, we needed meat for supper. We got it off two northern beauties, a fifteen-pounder and a twenty-pounder.

Last licks at fishing for the boys. For the botanists, last additions to complete their collection. I was busy with our estimated counts of the ducks we saw. There were so many of them and of other birds, we thought they must already be preparing for their great flights south. Daily since leaving Thicket Portage, we had seen double-crested cormorants. These diving fish-eaters average thirty inches in length and fly with their long necks outstretched. The Indians call them crow ducks.

Every evening the air was filled with the northland evening concert. Incessant cries of the terns, loons, and gulls were the chorus. Now and then a grand-daddy bullfrog chimed in with bass notes. The murmur of the water supplied the undertones. Sounds of nasal resonance came from nighthawks darting and diving overhead in great numbers.

Above the falls the Nelson widened rapidly to flow more placidly between low marshy shores, the shallows choked with a lush growth of water plants—wild rice, bulrushes, arrow-head, sedges and grasses. By midmorning we were approaching High Rock, where, seven weeks ago, we had veered off to the northeast and headed for God's Lake. We and our canvas Hudson Bay freighters had come full circle. On a map our route more nearly resembled a long-tailed kite. The tail, attached to the kite at High Rock, extended southward to Lake Winnipeg. From this point on we were retracing our steps.

15

Expedition's End

Shouts resounded from one canoe to another as we began to catch sight of familiar landmarks. "Hey, remember that?" "Look over there!" "Winnipeg, here we come!"

Our hilarity was jarred by the sight of a man out on the point of a small island some distance to our left. He was frantically waving and shouting.

"He's shouting at us, Chief! That guy's trying to stop us!" yelled Chuck.

We paddled over as fast as we could. The man was an Indian; he spoke no English. By gesture he directed us around the point of the island. There, lying partly submerged in a shallow bay, were two dead moose, a cow and a calf. The Cree had shot them as they stood out in the water feeding on lily tubers.

His wife and four small children stood silently on the shore, eying sadly and helplessly a supply of fresh meat that was so near and yet so far. The animals were much too large and too heavy to be dragged out of the water and brought in on shore to be dressed. Eleven white men with lots and lots of rope had come along just at the right time. The Indian was very happy. He grinned from ear to ear and grew quite excited as he directed operations. In no time the great brown bodies were lying on the rocks ready for the butchering.

At that point the Cree produced two hunting knives, drew them back and forth over his hand, shook his head sadly and proffered the edges for Ben to feel. They were dull. The white men came to the rescue with their honing stones.

With skill and gusto the Indian started to skin the calf. "Excuse me, please!" I gulped, and hurriedly turned my back. But those of our crew who had never before seen big game being dressed watched the process with fascination.

The little Indian pressed upon us both hind quarters of the calf in return for services rendered. "One is enough!" Ben tried to tell him.

We dug around to find enough candy bars to pass out to the whole family. They accepted them shyly, without a word or even a smile. But when Ben presented the oldest boy and the father with stones for sharpening their knives, their eyes fairly danced with pleasure. Here was something they valued far more than money or candy.

How different Sea River Falls looked to us as we

pulled in to make the lift-over. Less than two months ago, our green crew had approached it clumsily and with apprehension. Their struggle in unloading and carrying all those heavy boxes and stacks of duffel had been a mountainous task.

Those tons of freight that came over Sea River Falls at the start of the trip had now dwindled to six wood boxes, none of them heavy, two waterproof food bags, camping gear, personal packs and scientific equipment. All of it was tossed up over the lift-out in jig time.

Our noon meal that day could scarcely be called a lunch. Red meat! The first we had seen all summer. Moose steaks, dozens of them. Three skillets were filled, emptied, filled again and again. Expecting the flavor to be on the strong, gamy side, we were surprised to find that eating young moose was just like eating veal. There was no wild taste whatsoever. Such feasting took two hours instead of the one we had planned on allowing for the noon meal. Another hour had been lost helping the Indian with his kill. Time was precious. We had to hurry.

That would be the moment for Mike and Steve, the dishwashers, to remember that they had not put water on to heat. Belatedly, the kettle went over a dying fire. There was a scurry to help get the pile of plates scraped and stacked—and then the skillets were dumped into the dishwater first! I let out a wail of despair. "How often have I tried to tell you, *dishes first?* Now look!"

There was a floating layer of flakes of black soot and greasy slime so thick you couldn't see through it. Nothing to do but build up the fire, heat more water and start over again.

Ben remarked, "Marion, you'll just have to admit to being a dismal failure. You can't ever teach a man to wash dishes!"

Mike and Steve were incredibly cheerful. "You can't help it if we can't learn."

"Do you want to?"

They laughed out loud. "Nope."

With the unused portion of the meat wrapped in moss and covered to keep it cool and away from flies, we headed off. Hope Island, our goal, was still many miles and many hours away, but if we were to have that much-needed full day to get laundered and sorted out, we had to camp there this evening. We paddled on under a hot sun, and the calm became oppressive and breathless.

Then with no warning whatever, a head wind hit with such force that even with every ounce of push we had behind each stroke, we moved as though we were dragging anchors. To battle against the gale was a pure waste of time. It was foolish even to attempt to reach Hope Island. We headed for the nearest available camping spot.

"We've got to put the rest of today to good use," warned the Chief. "You can all start getting cleaned up right now. Those that are waiting for hot water can help me cut up and cook the rest of the moose meat. Got to keep it from spoiling."

Next day it was Norway House or bust. For three and a half hours we battled against that head wind to reach Hope Island. To escape the audience of curious onlookers we could expect to have around the post, we stopped here, a few miles short of Norway House, to finish washing clothes, scrub the canoes, air sleeping bags. At best we would probably not smell too sweet. The smoky aura that clings to clothes and dunnage, though not noticeable or objectionable to veteran campers, would no doubt have the tourists sniffing suspiciously.

At sundown we loaded and set out to cross little Playgreen Lake. The wind kicked up a rough sea. Choppy waves broke over the bow. Gallons of water sloshed in on us and our dunnage. It would be too much to expect to end the trip both clean and dry. By the time we reached Norway House we were very wet and it was dark. While tents were being pitched across the river from the Hudson's Bay Company's post, Ben paddled over to ask for mail. He returned with a nice stack, and by flashlight we eagerly tore open and read the first letters we had received since we left home.

A fine drizzle turned into an all-night heavy rain. "These tents will mildew before we have a chance to spread them out to dry." Snarkey could make a joke out of anything.

But the sun came out a few short hours before the boat was due, and we fell over each other trying to get things done. The contents of the food boxes and bags went in one pile to be given to the natives. Soot-blackened cook kettles were scoured, the chuck box scrubbed and sunned.

With twelve personal packs emptied, brushed, aired, and turned back to the Chief, there were clothes spread out over half an acre waiting to be crammed into "city luggage" that had been stored for us at the post. Suitcases contained the respectable clothes we had saved to get home. They were one solid mass of wrinkles.

The crew guffawed when they saw Steve in what had been a natty sports jacket. The shoulders were too tight, the sleeves too short. He had gained at least ten pounds; so had Snarkey. And Mike had grown leaner and broader.

"Look at the Runt! Almost grown!" chuckled Franklin. "He doesn't look like somebody's baby brother any more, he looks like he's wearing something that belongs to the brother."

"You don't look so hot yourself," Mike retorted happily. "Why don't you comb your hair?"

"Can't. It hasn't seen a comb for so long it's un-tamable. The barber in Winnipeg will just have to goo it down."

We carried the three canoes up to the warehouse for storage and covered the dunnage stacked on the dock. The sun disappeared again, and when a shrill

whistle announced the *Chickama,* another summer
shower was coming down in sheets. The whole Ferrier
crew stood on the dock in the rain and relayed tents,
bags, suitcases, packs and paddles to be stowed below deck. We boarded the launch drenched to the
skin.

On the tourist-packed little boat there was no
place to change. Well, being wet was nothing new.
Hadn't we known the feeling of wet clothes for days
on end? Hadn't we learned that continual attempts
to change just left us with three wet outfits instead
of one? What were dripping hair, shoes that squished
when we walked, clinging, soppy shirts and trousers
to us? We would "wear them dry" one last time.

Steve reported, "A nice old lady in the lounge just
now told me she was worried about us all getting
pneumonia before we get to Winnipeg! I'm afraid I
almost laughed in her face!"

Just at dinner time we reached Warren's Landing
at the head of Lake Winnipeg, piled off the launch,
and boarded the *S.S. Keenora,* ready to eat up the
profits of the company. And that night in our cabins
we all felt suffocated.

Just before the *Keenora* docked at Winnipeg
everybody rushed around pumping one another's
hands and saying all the things a crew like ours can

say in place of good-by. There wouldn't be much time for good-by once we had docked. There were barber shops to be visited and suits to have pressed and trains to be caught, to Chicago, Minnesota, and Iowa. This was the last chance for hashing over the expedition, for comparing tans and biceps, and for dreaming up possible future ventures on the trail. And for general round-table congratulations.

John and Orie had surpassed their goal of fifteen hundred plant specimens, without making anything like a complete study of the territory; they had never exhausted the possibilities of any location. The work they had done was not an isolated thing, but a small part of a long-term project. There would be years more of research by many other scientists.

"But we think we've accomplished what we set out to do," John said, with an affirmative nod from his partner. "Our contribution has a definite value—it'll help fill in one of the blank spots on the botanical map."

"And on top of that, I'm a new man!" Orie shook his head wonderingly. "I've absolutely amazed myself this summer. I started out as a classroom variety scientist. I wasn't at all sure I hadn't bitten off more than I could chew. And now I find I've performed all sorts of physical feats I thought I couldn't. Thanks to you, Chief."

Ben's comment was meant for everyone. "Thank yourself. Can't teach a man to do something he isn't capable of—or refuses to try."

It was Art's turn. "Walt and I have learned what we were after, all right. Now that we know what the great rivers and lakes are really like, we're going to navigate them ourselves another year, without having to come up with three meals a day for twelve hungry people!"

"Me, I could make a speech—but I won't," smiled Ben. "Except to say that this has been one of the best and most satisfying expeditions I've ever taken into the North. You all know already how I feel about nature, and woodsmanship; canoeing—sportsmanship—the crying need for conservation of all our natural resources and our wildlife; and the way the wilderness is bound to bring out what's in a man."

Snarkey murmured, "He's not going to make a speech," and the laugh was on the Chief.

Steve looked around at the crew. "Well, I don't know about the rest of you, but I don't think I can say anything truer than that I agree with the Chief, and I've had the experience of a lifetime."

There was a chorus of approval. "Black flies, bulldogs, and all. In spite of 'em, by golly. In spite of whales and high water."

"In spite of slaving till we're nothing but skin and bone." That drew another laugh. It was Piggy Dunbaugh speaking—one hundred eighty pounds and solid muscle.

"Yessir! The experience of anybody's lifetime."

It was Mike who had the last word. "Gee whiz! I thought it was just me, but the way you folks carry on, I think we've all come under the spell of the Witigo."

Nobody disagreed. The North country can do that to you.

Appendix

TWELVE PERSONAL PACKS

(20 x 24 x 6 inches. Woods bags, square-sided and having both shoulder and head straps.)

Clothing and equipment for each member of party.

toilet kit
1 suit long underwear (part wool)
3 suits summer weight underwear
3 pairs heavy wool socks
2 pairs light wool socks
1 pair cotton socks
1 heavy wool shirt
1 flannel shirt
1 cotton shirt
1 rain suit—waterproof trousers and jacket with parka hood
3 pairs mooseskin moccasins
2 pairs moccasin overs

1 pair tennis shoes
1 broad-brimmed felt hat
6 bandana kerchiefs
2 hand towels
1 bath towel
1 wash cloth
2 pairs cotton work trousers
1 pair wool trousers
1 pair heavy work gloves
1 head net
   sleeping bag
   air mattress (optional)
   insect repellent
   pocket knife
   waterproof match case
   fishing rod and reel
   fishing tackle (limit to cigar-box size)
   camera and film (optional)
   tumpline
1 pair flannel pajamas
   stationery
   diary

FOOD LIST

(12 men. 51 days)

  40 pounds pilot biscuits
  12 pounds soda biscuits
  50 pounds corn meal
 100 pounds white flour
  75 pounds powdered milk
  30 pounds pancake flour
   3 pounds baking powder
  10 pounds cocoa
  18 pounds coffee

   10 pounds tea
  100 pounds fresh potatoes
   15 pounds dehydrated potatoes
   36 pounds macaroni
   50 pounds prunes
   50 pounds dried apricots
   24 pounds pitted dates
   24 pounds salt
   ½ pound black pepper
   ½ pound cinnamon
  100 pounds white sugar
   25 pounds brown sugar
   40 pounds jam
   28 pounds honey spread
   12 pounds maple butter
   65 pounds butter (canned)
   25 pounds processed cheese
   20 pounds dried lima beans
   50 pounds dried navy beans
   18 pounds canned ham
   24 pounds canned roast beef
   50 pounds slab of bacon
   65 pounds canned bacon
   45 pounds dehydrated vegetables
   12 pounds graham crackers
   15 pounds salted peanuts
   25 pounds rice
   25 pounds raisins
   50 pounds oatmeal
   25 pounds caramels
   25 pounds candy bars (30 dozen)
   24 pounds shortening
   12 pounds peanut butter
    5 pounds dried peas

5 pounds dried apples
5 pounds dehydrated onions
5 pounds egg powder (15 packages)
½ pound baking soda
18 pounds pudding powders (6 dozen packages)
2 pounds lemon powder
60 dozen fresh eggs
50 loaves bread
12 packages dried yeast
4 bottles mapleine (2 ounces)
8 boxes matches
24 rolls toilet tissue
8 bars kitchen soap
5 cans scouring powder
10 yards kitchen toweling
5 scouring pads

FIRST AID KIT and MEDICAL SUPPLIES

band-aids
toothpick applicators
tongue depressors
cotton
1-inch adhesive
3-inch adhesive (5 yard roll) for sprains
2½-inch elastic bandage   "   "
2-inch gauze bandage
surgical gauze (5 yard roll)
scissors
tweezers
thermometer
1 ounce antiseptic
tourniquet
eye-dropper

finger cots
safety pins

aspirin tablets
zinc oxide ointment
burn ointment
anesthetic ointment
mentholatum
camphor ice
toothache drops
analgesic balm (aching muscles)
bismuth compound (diarrhea)
milk of magnesia tablets (indigestion)
alum (canker sores)
z b t powder (chafing and skin irritations)
aromatic spirits of ammonia (fainting)
boric acid crystals ⎫ (for hot wet compresses in case of
epsom salt crystals ⎭   infections)
hot water bag

ADDITIONAL EQUIPMENT—COMMUNAL

Tents: 2 4-man wall tents 7 x 9 feet; 2 2-man explorers tents 7 x 7 feet

Tarpaulins: 10 x 13 feet—one to each canoe

Axes: 1 long-handled Hudson Bay ax for wood supply; 1 short-handled grubbing ax for pitching tents

Watches: one to each canoe

Drinking cups: one tied to each canoe

Paddles: individual and one extra to each canoe

Flashlights: one to each tent

Tracking lines: 300 feet—one to each canoe

Lining ropes: 50 feet—one to each canoe.

Aerosol bombs: insect spray—one to each tent
Field glasses: 1 pair
Field guides: birds, plants, etc.
Compass
Sewing kit
Clothesline
Playing cards
Maps
Gun and ammunition for scientific collecting
Hunting knife
Canoe repair kit
Chuck box: 24 x 20 x 12 inches, constructed of wood
and divided into two compartments:
Upper compartment containing:
check list of food supplies
staples such as salt, pepper, tea, coffee, etc.
matches
makings for noon lunch to be added daily
Lower compartment containing:
nesting cook kit:
4 aluminum kettles
2 skillets
14 each: knives, forks, spoons
14 aluminum plates
14 enamel cups
reflector oven
pancake turner
can opener
knife sharpener
canvas water bucket
dish towels
soap
scouring powder
scouring pads